WALKING CARDIFF

WALKING CARDIFF

Peter Finch & John Briggs

SEREN

is the book imprint of
Poetry Wales Press Ltd.
57 Nolton Street, Bridgend, Wales, CF31 3AE

www.serenbooks.com
facebook.com/SerenBooks
twitter: @SerenBooks

© Peter Finch, 2019
Photographs © John Briggs, 2019

The right of Peter Finch to be identified
as the author of this work has been asserted
in accordance with the Copyright,
Designs and Patents Act, 1988.

ISBN 978-1-78172-558-0

A CIP record for this title is available
from the British Library.

The publisher works with the financial
assistance of the Welsh Books Council.

Cover photograph: Kevin Atherton's 'A Private View'.

Cardiff vector map courtesy of 4UMaps.

Printed by Bell & Bain Ltd, Glasgow.

CONTENTS

Rumney

St Fagans

Whitchurch

HOW TO USE THIS BOOK

The walks in this book have been arranged in alphabetical order by start point. Some are circular, most are linear. They are walks largely for the urban explorer rather than the yomper. At the time of writing they all follow legal and accessible routes. Trespass onto private land might offer short cuts but these are not recommended. Decent shoes and some rain protection are minimum requirements. Transport to and from routes is indicated in the book with many walks starting and ending at rail stations which makes everything accessible from the centre of Cardiff.

Route descriptions offer plenty for the armchair walker. Maps are provided, as are web links to Plotaroute, an online route planner at www.plotaroute.com. Here the precise routes followed have been recreated enabling walkers to check their progress on smartphones. This service is free. OS maps are best followed using the survey's own proprietary software at www.ordnancesurvey.co.uk/shop/mapfinder which can render both Landranger and explorer maps of Cardiff in high resolution. There is a charge for this service.

SHOW

Crewyd a llwyfannwyd gan **SLAVA**
Created and Staged by **SLAVA**

wmc.org.uk
029 2063 6464
Mae croeso i chi gysylltu â ni yn Gymraeg

HYDREF 17 – 21 OCTOBER

CANOLFAN
MILENIWM
CYMRU
WALES
MILLENNIUM
CENTRE

WHAT WILL YOU SEE IN CARDIFF?

IRIS PRIZE FESTIVAL
CARDIFF OCT 10-15 HYD CAERDYDD

MEDIA PARTNERS

      PARTNERS

WWW.IRISPRIZE.ORG

INTRODUCTION

There are a few things about a good walk. It should take you somewhere you haven't been before. It should get you lost and then it should find you. It should thrill you, excite you, inform you. It should get you to the end (or back to where you started) without overly killing you. And it should be memorable enough to have you tell others where you've been. The walks in this book are like that. All of them.

They are in Cardiff, set across an urban landscape where hikers rarely go, where the rucksacked with boots, walking poles and maps on cords are an uncommon sight. Cardiff, capital, financial centre, heart of government, education epicentre, European city (or so it tells us) and home for a new post-industrial urbanity that is expanding faster than anywhere else in Wales.

For now, though, the city remains containable, knowable, walkable. Confined by a ridge of hills focused on Caerphilly mountain to the north and by the Severn Sea to the south it is barely 7 miles across. A lozenge of a municipality where you can reach most places on foot, if you want to, where the parks and urban woodlands are many and the hills are few and where you can readily become familiar with everywhere and then still get lost.

As a place to live it fancies itself as a modernist paradise. New build in gushes going on everyplace, tower blocks rising right across the centre, new districts of town houses emerging out of the farmland on the fringes. The apartment blocks facing the tamed and barraged bay are made to look like liners. Porthole windows, balconies like cruiser decks, white gleam in the seagull-filled air. Our maritime past uniquely celebrated except it isn't really. Cross the UK and you'll find off the peg redevelopment much like Cardiff's going on everywhere.

But we do punch above our weight. Just slightly. As the capital of a small nation we have acquired all the right and relevant accoutrements. Ready transport access to the rest of the UK, opera house, national museums and sports stadia, the government parliament buildings, universities almost beyond number, national administrative hubs and a clubland to die for. If you want to die. Do some of the city centre walks on a Friday night after 11.00 pm and you'll see what I mean.

Cardiff is nothing like it used to be. Before the war (and for quite a while after) this was a dark place. There was coal in the streets, outsiders claimed, although it was never quite that bad. It did, however, focus on two of the dirtiest businesses known to industrial man – steel making and coal exporting. The docks, all five of them, welcomed ship after ship, all to be filled with black dust-producing showers of valley anthracite shovelled and poured from coal staithes, filling the fresh Bristol Channel air with powdered slack. Most of the south of the city that wasn't engaged in this business made steel instead. Gouts of steam and smoke, noise and fire raining daily staining everything they touched. Workers sat in the pubs after their exhausting shifts unable to speak. Three pints. At least. Get the muck from our throats.

All that has gone. The whole wasteland it left behind is now largely cleared, repaired and replaced with a gleaming glass and aluminium future. Millennials have always known the city like this, of course. For them heavy industry is a rumour, fanned by 'old Cardiff' articles in the papers and letters to postbag. Born after 2000 they have never known the dirt and the toil with which this place once filled itself. For them it has always been Barrage and Millennium Centre, Principality Stadium and a townscape of multiplex and bar.

The best way to see this new city is not by bus which goes where it goes, nor by car from which it is so hard to see and, given the ubiquity of double yellow, can't stop and stay pretty much anywhere. It might be by bike, on which you'll be invisible and able to enter almost any space. But best would be on foot, boldly going, able to look at anything and everything, fancy a coffee have one, and worry-free at your destination where no one will steal your cycle from the pole you've locked it against nor bash your car with a misguided trolley in the car park at Tesco where you've left it for the max allowed two hours. Most of the walks in this book will take just a bit longer than that anyway.

If psychogeography is anything then it is the art of visiting places where you might otherwise not go. Experiencing the sense a place has, its spirit, its essence which hangs in the air. If it is a land of bungalows, how many are blue, let's walk along every lane, why not take a left turn just to see what's there, what will a tourist make of the non-tourist wonders of suburban dérive[1]? If, as Baudelaire suggested, all city dwellers suffer from a sort of anxious alienation then how might that feel? How many parks has Cardiff got? Let's visit as many as we can. Let's visit them all.

Council housing, Llanedeyrn Estate

Naturally the municipal authorities have come up with their own trails, guiding visitors around the historic high spots (Castle, City Hall, St John's Church) and showing them the gleaming new (Barrage, WMC, Senedd). Printed guides sporadically available. All great stuff but don't anticipate too much of that family day out tourist trailing in this book. Expect instead a set of walks that largely follow the principles outlined at the start of this introduction. We go where others generally do not. We look for the different. We explore the less visited. We cross the city's dormitory estates to discover what's on the other side. We tour poetry's revolutionary Cardiff centres. We visit the houses of the great north Cardiff novelists. We track where railways once were. We follow rivers and explore urban woodlands. We check out how the well-to-do manage as much as we do the less well off.

Over the past two decades I've written four books that explore Cardiff's real side (and in the process spawned a series that does the same for other urbanities first across Wales and now the rest of the UK). In the process I've found that the single best way to get to know a place is to walk across it. Read its histories and check its maps (old and new), sure. But get out there and check the way the streets actually run. Why were they put just here? What's along them? What might have been here before? Are there any traces? On Cardiff's great river delta of a cityscape so much can be discerned just by looking.

The Cardiff Bay shore

The current book is a workable and walkable guide presented so that the reader can go just where we've been, read what we've found and then make discoveries of their own. No walk here should whap you. All start and end in sensible places with public transport readily available. Cardiff is good at that, despite what you might hear about how it used to be. We do buses well, they go everywhere. Soon the railways, in the form of the expanding Cardiff Metro with its light rail trams, will follow them.

Diesel Sprinter Unit approaches Coryton

The method employed was to check Google Earth and then design a workable ramble, often using Plotaroute and detailed OS maps in paper form and then on my phone's OS Mapfinder. Finding out where you are is no longer the challenge it once was. I'd then walk bits to ensure they worked (just because it shows a path on the map does not necessarily mean one is actually there) and finally I tracked the whole route in the company of fellow psychogeographer, industrial remains enthusiast and fan of Morris dancing, trains and real ale, the photographer John Briggs.

John's forte is catching the spirit of a place and its people. His photographs are post-industrial wonders. I'd walk and take notes. John would walk and snap. We'd go through what we'd uncovered and collected and then edit hard. The results complete with route maps rendered by Jamie Hill are here. Not quite do it yourself Real Cardiff but near enough.

But the city evolves, continues to do this daily. In fact not since its great nineteenth century period of heroic expansion has the city boomed like it is booming now. Get out there and look at it yourself before it all changes once again and you'll need to buy *Cardiff Walking Two*. Onwards we go.

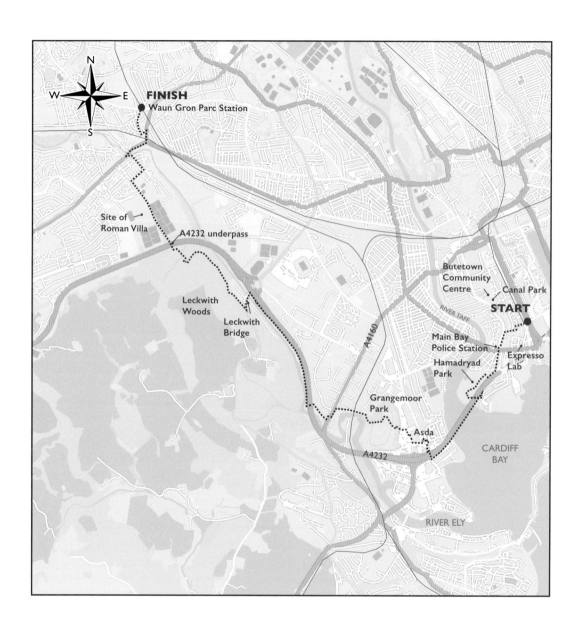

1. CARDIFF BAY TO WAUN GRON PARK

A walk across post-industrial Cardiff checking how the scars have healed. Spectacular views across Cardiff Bay and a lush trek along the River Ely below Cock Hill. On through Leckwith Woods to cross the lost Ely Racecourse with its Roman villa. The walk ends at Waun Gron Park railway station in Fairwater. An exhilarating and very varied walk replete with public artworks, woodland trees and kingfishers.

Start: Cardiff Bay Rail Station
Finish: Waun Gron Park Rail Station
Distance: 6.13 miles
Mostly level, incline across Grangemoor Park and onto the lower reaches of Cock Hill

www.plotaroute.com/route/542405

Pre-industrial Cardiff was a lot nearer the sea than the present post-industrial version. A combination of sequential land reclamation, estuarine silt and dredging has pushed the coast a lot nearer to Bristol than it was a thousand years ago. That was when Robert Fitzhamon and his Normans came over to build their stone castle on the plundered remains of Cardiff's Roman Fort. I'm walking with John along the rim of where that earlier Cardiff coast may well have been. I can't be sure. Before Speed's map of 1610 nobody seems to have marked anything down.

It's cold enough to freeze the ink in my Biro but we are undaunted. I've caught the train down the single track from Queen Street. It's been a rush of commuters, ear phones, rucksacks, and coffee in double the size they were when I was a kid, carriable, lidded, unrecyclable cups. John has walked from Central. Fifteen minutes he says, his ears coddled in a woollen hat and his feet encased in new, totally waterproof, easy on your feet fell trekkers.

Cardiff Bay Station is at the terminus of what was the Taff Vale Railway's multi-tracked route into Bute Road, a splendid Georgian-looking one-time many platformed station that had the TVR Board Room and the offices of a whole string of consulates next door. The TVR engine works were over the road.

Former Taff Vale Railway station and company board rooms, Bute Street

We cross Bute Street to enter West Close, passing the currently closed Butetown Community Centre and Gardens built onto the site of the old slipper baths[2]. As part of the re-branding of Butetown artist Nina Edge and ceramist David Makie have been employed to create a circular art work and gardens, as a place to "show off, sit, play, chew ghat, smoke weed and meet[3]". This they've done, providing a neat red brick court yard with a huge decorated disc at its centre. In the archives there's an iconic photograph of a pre-grouping[4] TVR engine sitting on a turntable right at this spot. Not that today any memory of engines or railways remains. The small housing development that has replaced the industry is neat and silent. A bloke in a puffa jacket crosses in headphones and rucksack and carrying the ubiquitous coffee. Freezing rain starts to fall.

We exit through the Close's end onto what's now Canal Park but in its heyday was the Glamorgan Canal Basin, Cardiff's first sea dock. Bert Hardy photographed kids skimming stones here in 1950 a year before the sand dredger *Catherine Ethel* collided with the sea lock gates tearing them off and draining the whole Canal Pond, it turns out, forever. There are a couple of bollards around which hawsers once tied barges unloading iron and coal. As part of a community arts project they have had their tops painted white and lettered with the words 'Home Sweet Home'.

We divert briefly through the increasing drench to view the restored Ballast Bank, a stylised public art creation on which stands a silver lighthouse with a blue lamp on top. This is 'The Blue Beacon' installed by Renn & Thacker in 2009. It is located outside the main Police Station and the words engraved onto the stones are redolent of Cardiff Docks' communities, industries, places and people. They are my own composition. "Pirate, Portuguesa, Petroleum, Polski" the text runs. Among them, in the same blue lettering, someone recently added the words "All Coppers Are Bastards". Cleaned off now, when I look. The Chief Constable wanted something appropriate she could be filmed standing beside, like that slowly turning triangular structure outside New Scotland Yard. Not that I've ever seen the Blue Beacon on television. Clearly not media friendly enough.

Cymreigiad Cymraeg

Hebraeg Heddgeidwad

Native Nobiin Naval

Stock dalian

Back along James Street, beyond what was until recently the Bay's last genuine dock tavern, the White Hart – now Irie Shack Caribbean Bar and Grill – we duck into Espresso Lab. This is a welcome and warm coffee shop on the site of Williams Shipping Chemists and next door to Atlas Chambers. The store's rear is collaged with old photos of Butetown and the Bay. Loudon Square, the Carnival, marching jazz bands, Bay schoolchildren in Welsh costume, local teacher and activist Betty Campbell meeting the young Prince Charles, kids on swings. John stares. "Some of these images are mine," he says. "Used without permission." They have been lifted mainly from his great collection of Bay photographs taken in the 1970s, *Before The Deluge*. "Does this upset you?" I ask. "Not really. It happens. What can you do?"

Once the rain has slowed enough to allow progress we return to the track of the canal and walk south past the Royal Stuart Wharf workshops and the roundhouse of Mount Stuart Primary school. The 1994 memorial to the site of the Sea Lock recalls a colourful dockland past but it's not quite in the right spot. The gates themselves sat out where the A4232 link road emerges from the Butetown Tunnel. Not that this really matters. History is always an approximate thing.

We cross through the bottom edge of Hamadryad Park, an extended expanse that has been windswept and largely deserted every time I've visited since its creation in 2001. The mudbanks onto which the hulk of *HMS Hamadryad* was hauled in 1866 to create an isolation hospital ship for sick seamen are currently being redeveloped as community housing.

We walk under the slim bulk of the 1995 Link Road bridge that soars over the Taff Estuary and get onto it using the steps on the southern side. These take us to a path with spectacular views across the Bay to the Barrage and beyond. Dock cranes, serried yachts, the Barrage's bascule bridges, the dark bulk of Penarth Head, the sunlit gleam of Flat Holm, ship-shaped St David's Hotel, the white sides of the Norwegian Church, a whole Bayscape shining. The rain has stopped falling now but it's still being rushed up in great clouds by passing 70 mph container lorries.

On the Ely side the crossing is celebrated with a giant silver ball, Kevin Atherton's 1995 artwork, 'A Private View'. A life-size bronze figure of a businessman peers inside. Visitors are invited to do the same, viewing the Norwegian Church on the Bay's far side. But today the structure sits in a vast pool of rainwater. John and I photograph our own funfair distorted reflections in the ball's curving silver sides.

We descend, a welcome respite from the flying road slosh to reach Ferry Road. South leads to the land of still under-construction snowdomes, hotels, skyscraper casinos and swimming pools. Cardiff Council's Sports Village. We head north instead along what was once the line of the Penarth Harbour & Dock railway. We go through Cardiff Candle Works and Imperial Wharf, now Asda car park, to climb the mound of the reclaimed west Cardiff landfill. This has been rebranded as Grangemoor Park, *Asda Park* to locals. 'Silent Links', Ian Randall's sculpture of anchor chain and lost industry sits right on top. This whole landscape has been re-trieved from a onetime oxbow on the River Ely. Views are all encompassing. A whole still developing sky-reaching city to the north, Penarth's headland west and the Severn Estuary's seascape rolling on out to Ireland.

After sliding about in the mud streams that populate the sides of the mound in bad weather we reach what the Council's Outdoor Cardiff Department have designated as a waymarked path – the seven mile Ely Trail north all the way to St Fagans. But we won't be going that far.

As a trail this is a splendid idea, river peace to the left on the northern trek, a biodiversity of greenness, herons, king-fishers, bluebells and wild garlic. But marred on the right by having the constant thunder of that Link Road running at touchable distance. For respite you get inside your head and stay there. Best Buddhist proof against the modern world. The walk is a mile's worth. We cross Penarth Road at Cardiff Marine Village. There is a slipway here, direct onto the Ely, pleasure boats stacked three high like some sort of maritime multi-story car park. Cardiff's shipping heritage reborn but not in the way that Bute might have imagined.

The 1536 Ely Bridge

We eventually emerge from the Ely Trail to cross the river on the Leckwith Bridge (or, as it's proudly labelled on the commemorative plaque from the time of its opening, 'Viaduct'). This structure (ribbon cut in 1935 by Leslie Hore-Belisha, he of the flashing beacons) replaces an earlier medieval three-arched stone structure from 1536. This is actually still there in full tarmac-topped use below us. It leads to Leckwith Woods. Behind it are the once empty moorlands criss-crossed with hopeful drainage ditches that ran back to where Ninian Park came to be built. Beyond were the Canton engine sheds of the GWR. Today it's a mass of retail park and stadia, Cardiff Athletic, Cardiff City Football Club, the sports goods stores of DW Fitness, M&S, Costco, and the rest of the usual suspects.

The small corner of land nestling in the woods that the medieval bridge reaches is entirely in the hands of conurbation edgeland dwellers, independents hacking a living out of things others don't want to do – scaffolders, plant management operators, construction companies, concrete block makers – although there is a sign announcing the arrival soon of new housing as the city continues to blossom.

The Cardiff boundary with the Vale is here, announcing its presence at the start of the hill road but we don't cross that magic line. We stick, instead, to the level path through the greenery that rolls upriver. This is deep woodland, the river invisible behind scrub, beech and oak in great stands. But this is deciduous winter and here's little to hold back the low throb of traffic that filters through from that Link Road. Not that any of this is disconcerting, we simply don't listen.

Above us, at slope top and totally out of sight, is Bryn Ceiliog (which translates as Cock Hill) and the Cardiff vineyards of Ian Symonds. Both red and white have been made and are more than palatable (See *Real Cardiff Three*) although production is, through indisposition, currently temporarily suspended. The path slants down to pass an abandoned and now moss-covered Ferro-concrete storage tank, metal access ladders, pipework, drains, sunk into the mud like something from one of J.G. Ballard's end of the world dystopias. A woodland interpretation board, wrecked and pockmarked with gunshot, announces the proximity of a housing estate. Highlighting this the path dips through a richly-graffitied underpass to emerge at the southern end of western Cardiff's greatest of open spaces – Trelai Park.

This expanse with its myriad football pitches, not a single one actually in use today, was built on the site of Cardiff's Ely Racecourse. This racecourse superseded an earlier one at the Heath and was in use from 1855 until the 1950s, offering a home to sheepdog trials as well as the Welsh Grand National. We cross the racecourse's southern straight which today, as a swathe of mown grass, points out across the city towards the distant Pearl Building (now Capitol Tower, Greyfriars Road, for decades until the Meridian Quay Tower in Swansea beat it, Wales' tallest structure).

In the park's centre is an unmarked hummocky square of rough ground, grass-covered but not tightly mown. If you didn't know you'd imagine this to be an eco-installation, a slab of land left for the buzzing of insects and the scattering of meadow flowers. The park authorities have chosen not to install an interpretation board. They know the fate of such things in Western Cardiff.

This is actually not the site of a monastery that nineteenth century locals thought it was but a Roman Villa. Sir Mortimer Wheeler excavated here in the 1920s. At two metres down he found mosaics, a bath house, iron workings, graves and a selection of pottery shards. A Roman road exited the villa site north to run like an arrow towards Ely Bridge.

At the park's far gates is Caerau Ely ABC boxing gym decorated with larger than life paintings of boxers and fire-breathing dragons together with what turns out to be the area's only celebration of the Roman presence – a centurion with sword drawn charging into battle.

We wind through Littlecroft Avenue and Dyfrig Road, passing the works of the Cardiff Lift Company to find the river again, in flood today. It is crossed by a bridge carrying Cowbridge Road West along with a brand-new tubular steel foot and cycle path structure. Passing the 1894 White Lion we follow the A48 to skirt the junction and access Ely Road and The Railway Hotel. Here, in the winter cold, a gang of East Europeans are washing cars with gouts of freezing foam. John snaps. Ever smiling, it seems, the parka-clad workers pose.

We are at one of Cardiff's many internal borders. Ely edges here into more upmarket Fairwater. The border is actually the river but the feel hardly shifts until you are well beyond it. Ahead is a green triangle made by the railway and the Fairwater Brook. A model of this constructed by Paul Rolley featured on BBC4's 2013 *The Joy Of (Train) Sets*. Fame at last. This is our destination. Waun Gron Park. It's hardly more than a big back garden really, but well-tended with benches and bins. On its far side is the welcome Radyr to Coryton City Line Rail Station. Newspaper shop selling chocolate bars and drinks in cans. Seats. Shelter. Regular diesels to Central. A fitting return and, if you wanted, on right back to where we started in Cardiff Bay.

The view from Ian Randall's *Silent Links*

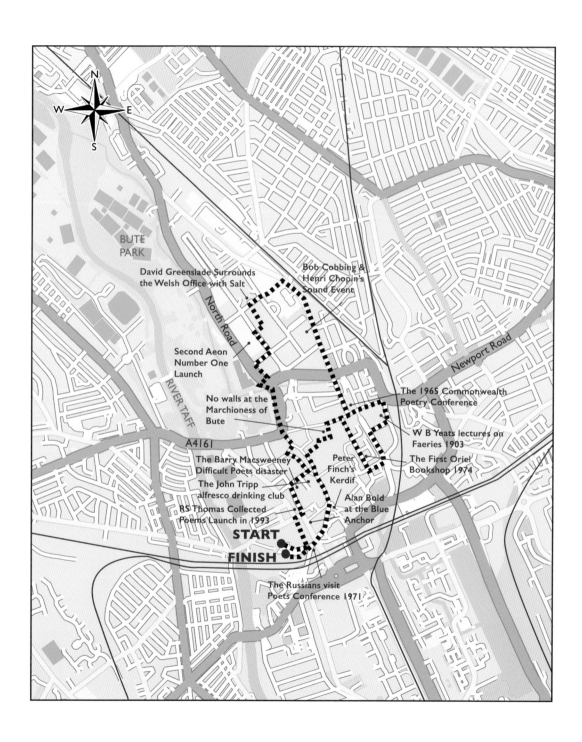

BUTE
PARK

David Greenslade Surrounds
the Welsh Office with Salt

Bob Cobbing &
Henri Chopin's
Sound Event

North Road

Second Aeon
Number One
Launch

RIVER TAFF

The 1965 Commonwealth
Poetry Conference

No walls at the
Marchioness of
Bute

A4161

Newport Road

W B Yeats lectures on
Faeries 1903

The Barry Macsweeney
Difficult Poets disaster

Peter
Finch's
Kerdif

The First Oriel
Bookshop 1974

The John Tripp
alfresco drinking club

RS Thomas Collected
Poems Launch in 1993

Alan Bold
at the Blue
Anchor

START

FINISH

The Russians visit
Poets Conference 1971

2. A CARDIFF COUNTER CULTURE POETRY RAMBLE

A circular literary walk around central Cardiff visiting sites associated with the poetry of the 60s and 70s counter culture. The ground-breaking and the revolutionary in the centre of the capital.

Start and finish: Cardiff Central Station
Distance 2.97 miles
Level

www.plotaroute.com/route/593496

Sometimes the intellectual focus of a place is hard to discern. Cardiff lacks the literary heat of places like Dublin or London or Edinburgh. Our poets, our famous ones, all seem to leave. R.S. to the north, Dannie Abse to Golders Green, Gillian Clarke to her bwthyn in Ceredigion. Only the first National Poet, Gwyneth Lewis, stays the course, up there in Penylan, detecting poetry wherever she can.

But in the late 60s something happened. The counter culture arrived and the world did some shaking. The city's poetry core changed forever. I'm walking with John tracking this revolution. It's a great three mile ramble looking for ghosts.

Outside the rail station where we begin there once stood a bronze sculpture of dubious origin. Its job was to welcome visitors to the capital. It squatted like a brown shoebox. Its sides were covered with randomly sourced quotes from the Anglo-Welsh cannon. It made no Cardiff sense but there it sat adding literary weight to English-speaking Wales. But in the station redevelopment it's been swept. Melted, I hope. Gone.

We walk up Great Western Lane towards the Prince of Wales, once a theatre on whose boards stepped Richard Burton, Noel Coward and Vivien Leigh, but now a Weatherspoon's pub. Opposite is the Royal Hotel with O'Neill's Bar occupying the whole ground floor. It is where that long-departed son of the city, R.S. Thomas, returned to launch his *Collected Poems* in 1993. He gave a typically expressionless and dour recital, as ever troubling Welsh consciousness with reminders of our status, our language and our soul.

Outline of St Mary's at the rear of The Prince of Wales Wetherspoons

Thomas's counter-culture credentials rest with his controversial support for the cottage burners and his opposition to most things that arrived from over the border. His poems radiated stubborn nationalism. A Welsh renegade in a suit and a dog collar. Paradoxically he wrote his often bitter verse in the language of the conqueror, English. The queue to buy a signed copy snaked right round the room and out down the stairs.

Our route on is up St Mary Street until the Sandringham Hotel appears on the right. Dating from the 1880s The Sandringham started life as an inn called The Black Lion. Look up and you'll see a stone lion still present on the top of the building. As the Sandringham Hotel it spent most of the twentieth century offering reasonably priced accommodation for weekend visitors, sales reps and wedding guests. In 1995 the hotel opened Café Jazz on its ground floor. This offered nightly music for the discerning with free admission for those who bought a meal. As a venue it still operates today. The poet Barry MacSweeney read here in the 1990s as part of an Oriel Bookshop-promoted series perceptively entitled *Difficult Poets*. The critic Nicholas Johnson called MacSweeney "a contrary, lone wolf, self-styled the 'prince of Sparty Lea[5]' who had been proscribed from official records of poetry for 25 years." His poetry, post-Prynne and linguistically enveloping, is among the best left field UK work British poets have produced.

Barry MacSweeney at the
Sandringham Hotel, St Mary's Street

On the night of the reading, a rare one for him, he'd hit the bottle. He arrived slurring and sliding and allowed a half empty vodka bottle to roll from his briefcase onto the floor in front of the dais. He then proceeded to read the same poem eight times offering, as a finale, a swinging of the microphone round his head as if he were a cowboy trying to lasso a steer. The gig was done for, the *Difficult Poets* series abandoned, and punters (the place was full of fans) all given their money back. MacSweeney died in 2000.

Turning right onto Wharton Street we access the southern end of the old Library. This is Hayes Island, a place known as Little Troy[6] back in the days of the early town. Until comparatively recently Hayes Island was home to a tea and cheese roll stall set up in what was once Cardiff Trams' parcel depot. During pale dry afternoons the Poets Alfresco Drinking Club met here. Led by John Tripp and supported by Robert Minhinnick and Nigel Jenkins the club offered a respite from literary matters (usually morning meetings of the Welsh Academy) to poets unable to gain sustenance in Cardiff's pubs. These were closed by law between 2.30 and 6.30. For most of the twentieth century drinking regulation did not favour the consumer. By the late 1980s things had relaxed somewhat and by 2002 'we never shut' licences were commonplace but by then JT had passed on and Academy afternoon meetings had gone the way of the mining industry.

The walk north through St John's Square and then onto Kingsway hustles through the city's real centre. Shoppers, skateboarders, buggy pushers, beggars, buskers. North of Kingsway we use the underpass to emerge at the edge of the Law Courts. To the north, slipping through City Hall Road is King Edward VII Avenue, done in red tarmac and as regal as it is overstuffed with parked cars. This is Cathays Park, the famous Portland Stone Civic Centre. To our left and just beyond the University Registry is the Glamorgan Building. It is now the School of Geography and Planning but in 1966 it was Glamorgan County Hall. I worked here. Clerk and poet. My idea was to change the world with verse, to usher in a brand new era, a second aeon of edge-pushing creativity where poets would show us all how to live. The fabulous excesses of youth.

Second Aeon Number One was foolscap, six duplicated pages on 64-mil old gold yellow. Selling price 3d. The poetry it gathered was mostly written by its editor. I stood in the corridor that ran between the Treasurer's Department and the Glamorgan Archives' photocopier and offered my wares. Over two lunchtimes I sold a hundred.

The way in is now called the South Entrance. 'Intercom. Press and wait for an answer.' Today it's as near as we'll get. *Second Aeon* went on to become one of the leading counter-culture poetry magazines of the era. It achieved an international readership fomenting change as it went. It ran for 21 issues.

Second Aeon celebrated outside the Glamorgan Building, Cathays Park

I look back at Albert Hodge's larger-than-life heroic statues guarding the entrance to the former County Hall and wonder why I barely noticed these incredibly impressive things when I worked here. Huge tridents, giant horses, sandaled feet in size 93.

We cross through neat and memorial-filled Alexandra Gardens to face the Welsh Office at the northern end. This neoclassical structure was surrounded with salt in a performance by the poet David Greenslade in 1996. He wanted to al-chemically purify the HQ of the colonial English much in the way American war protestors had when they surrounded the White House with flowers. He bought his salt sale or return at Safeway. "If you don't use it all, love, you can bring the rest back." A few years later the great referendum voted for greater Welsh self-determination and the Welsh Office transformed itself into a civil service centre for the incoming Welsh Government. The acts of poets sometimes work.

Taking the lane that turns alongside Cardiff University the route passes Rio Architects' Multi-coloured Swapshop South Podium for the Cardiff School of Biosciences. Its hexagonal coloured and internally lit panels are a startling and uplifting fit. On Park Place we head south until the curved frontage of the Museum's Reardon Smith Lecture Theatre appears on our right. This 300-seater and by now august venue has been home to a thousand events and not a few relating to the counter culture. The establishment facil-itating the anti-establishment. It's how our society works.

In 1970 Bob Cobbing and Henri Chopin came here for *A Sound Event*. Cobbing, master of verbivocovisual verse, brought roaring life to the smudged lists, typewriter wastage and scraps of ripped newspaper he held in his hand. Chopin recorded his breath on a Grundig tape recorder and then interfered with the playback using a stiffener pulled out of his shirt collar. This was Poésie Sonore. It soared. The per-formance proceeded for hours. The audience were stunned, entertained and enthralled. I would like to report that this startling and massively inventive display of new poetry then ushered in a new era of expanded Anglo–Welsh consciousness and catholic verse. But somehow it did not.

Park Place passes the Burges designed Park House (1874), crosses Boulevard de Nantes, and then moves south alongside The Park Hotel. Actually no longer the Park, sadly, but Jury's Inn with the site of some of its illustrious past rebranded as Oddsocks Bar and Kitchen. The new name implies that bohemians might be welcome here but my guess is they wouldn't be. They were not either in 1965 when this was one of the venues for Commonwealth Arts Festival Poetry Conference. Anthony Brockway at Babylon Wales describes the conference as a turbulent affair. "There were bust-ups, walk-outs, accusations of hooliganism, and an incident involving a Vietnamese pig." The poets, who included Jeff Nuttall, Brian Patten, Alexander Trocchi, George Macbeth, Mike Horovitz, Adrian Henri and Wole Soyinka, ran riot at the Park, keeping the bar in action until the early hours, pushing guests' shoes down lift shafts and scrawling obscenity-laden verse on the hotel's walls. The justification that this was performance art celebrating the dawning of a new age went nowhere. Park Hotel management were not impressed.

We turn left onto Queen Street which is in full Saturday flow. Street traders sell bird whistles, wall hangings, bubble guns, inflatable Spider Men and Welsh flags which double as tote bags. We walk as far as the branch of Greggs at the foot of what was once the AA Building but is now apartments. There are a couple of hopeful tables outside indicating that Greggs is setting its sights higher than they once were.

This is Station Terrace with Queen Street as the station and all stops to the Valleys the usual destination. Along here opposite the station's current entrance is the rear of the Capitol Centre, in use as a multi-story and a branch of the cut price Premier Cinema. Before these structures arrived in 1990 it was the Cory Hall. W.B. Yeats was here in 1903 reading poetry and talking about the Irish Faery Kingdom, the counter culture of that decade for sure. Yeats had been invited by the Welsh Society at University College as part of a consciousness-raising exercise. The Irish, as ever, managed their cultural revival well ahead of ours.

W B Yeats revisits Cardiff's Cory Hall on Station Terrace

We follow Edward Street, once the back way into the Capitol Cinema where the Beatles played in 1965, to turn south on Churchill Way. On the far side stood a jazz club which in the late 1980s was host to the great blues singer Jimmy Witherspoon, on his last legs with throat cancer and then the following night to Ifor Thomas, Tôpher Mills and members of the performance poetry troupe Cabaret 246. Poetry delivered late night to an inebriated student audience who were there for the cheap beer rather than the loud verse. Never has so much poetry been shouted at so many deaf ears. But it was how the form developed its stage presence and its ability to entertain whatever the noises off.

We are now bound for Charles Street, round the corner, where in 1974 at no 53 the first Oriel Bookshop opened. Today that crumbling building on the corner of Wesley Lane has gone. It has been replaced with a new brick set of offices for the Careers Service, itself due to be replaced with a high-rise in the not too distant. Until the nineteen nineties, however, when the shop moved to more expensive premises on the Friary, this was the centre of the Welsh Lit universe and where you came for any poetry book published anywhere in the Western world. Litterateurs flocked and not just those from the fringes although, it has to be said, the edge pushers were often first in line. Tom Raworth, John James, Bob Cobbing, Wendy Mulford, Fiona Pitt Kethley, Les Murray, Ken Smith, Eugene Ionesco, Lawrence Ferlinghetti, Andrew Motion, Simon Armitage, and Jeff

The Bookshop Manager at the site of Oriel Charles Street

Nuttall were among the many hundreds of luminaries who appeared here performing among paintings by the likes of Ivor Davies and Ernest Zobole, demolishing maquettes by accident (D.M. Thomas), burning the rubber legs of one of Allen Jones' rubber women (John Tripp) and having audience members faint and be passed to the open air over the heads of the crowds football match style (R.S. Thomas). There should be a plaque.

At the top of Charles Street beyond Denis O'Connor and Bernie Rutter's 'Without Place', a stainless steel sculpture to the street's early origins, we turn left on Queen Street to find the stubby remains of Frederick Street. This was originally a main route into the mesh of terraces and back to back houses that filled Cardiff's core. Slum cleared in the 60s. Almost entirely covered by shopping mall today. Just before the street bumps to a pointless end at the rear doors of Trespass we pass the staff entrance into Boots. The site of the Marchioness of Bute. Built in 1846 the pub lasted until the 1970s. The No Walls Poetry Readings were here, weekly on Wednesdays through 1968 into 1969. They hosted everyone from the legendary American sound poet Jackson Mac Low to Alan Perry balancing poems on his nose. It was here that Penguin Modern Poets Brian Patten and Adrian Henri thrilled the crowds and Alan Jackson demystified Scotland. Dave Stringer, Herbert Williams, Jim Burns and John Tripp were regulars.

The easiest way on is to enter the St David's Centre via Trespass, admire their collection of easy to wear anoraks and sweat pants and then follow the St David's shopping mall until you reach the Old Library. If this turns out to be difficult then the route is back up Frederick Street, left on Queen Street, and then right into St John's Square.

South of the Old Library, passing the other side of JT's Alfresco Drinking Club, The Hayes reaches Cardiff's legendary chip alley, Caroline Street. Opposite where the pointed prow of John Lewis meets the new Library and set in the paving beneath Jean Bernard Metais's great ring and spike is my own acrostic concrete poem composed from the variations of the city's name as they appeared in historical records. 'KERDIF' it reads, and then 'C ar di ff e'. Slices of Cardiff verse were to be displayed by projector mounted at the spike's top but the project's budget overran. Instead, and in an effort to salvage something, sections of the text – "Sabrina Afon Hafren / Severn solid / Sandy Roman frith" – can be read (in a good light) on the Library's window.

The determined will now follow Caroline Street and turn left onto lower St Mary Street to locate the site of the Blue Anchor. Today it's the BE AT ONE Cocktail Bar but in 1969 it was a far more old fashioned place. The Scottish poet and MacDiarmid expert Alan Bold came here to launch his new collection *A Pint of Bitter*. He'd already doorstepped Harold Wilson with his previous book, *The*

Kerdif – the Finch acrostic on the Hayes

State of the Nation, and was sure that pretty soon, the Prime Minister being a poetry lover, his ideas would appear in political manifesto. But for now it was poetry and beer. The drinkers at the Blue Anchor rallied. All was well, with Bold in mid flow, when the landlord announced that the pub's ancient cellar had flooded and further pints of bitter were now impossible. Bold retreated, drinkers in tow, through the early Cardiff terraces looking for a port in his beerless storm. He alighted on the Moulders Arms on Union Street where, welcomed by the landlord, he carried on. Bold died young in 1998. The Moulders went down a little earlier. Its spirit hangs on somewhere there below the pharmacy department in Boots.

The Bold-avoiders will have taken the easy way on down Mill Lane, once the route of the Glamorgan Canal, to face The Clayton Hotel with Viva Brazil Churrascaria on its ground floor. The Central Hotel stood here until, derelict, it was mysteriously destroyed by fire in 2003. A venue for any number of great events it hosted a grand meeting of Poets Conference, a sort of UK-wide trade union for bards, in 1971. The luminaries came to argue for more cash – "Bread on the Night" as Adrian Henri suggested. George Macbeth, Jeff Nuttall, Bob Cobbing, Alison Bielski, Bryn Griffiths,

Glyn Jones were among the delegates. They were joined by a visiting group of Soviets. Four Russian poets (plus their KGB minder and a translator) including Mikhail Dudin, Georgi Dmitrievich Gulia, the Georgian Editor of the official magazine of the Soviet Writer's Union, *Literanaya Gazeta*, Supreme Soviet member Sergei Narovchatov, and the Belarusian and marvellously named Maksim Tank. They were here to see how our workers got on. Outside the miners were marching down St Mary Street in search of better wages. Inside the poets were arguing for better fees. The Soviets all had cut-outs of the feet of their family members and details of their chest measurements in their jacket pockets. When we were done they set off directly to Marks & Spencer's and shops that sold Clarks. It had been a day of socialism in action. The poets glowed. The miners rested. The Russians all had new shoes.

Ahead, up Saunders Road, is the Central Station again. Full circle.

The 1971 Central Hotel Poet's Conference

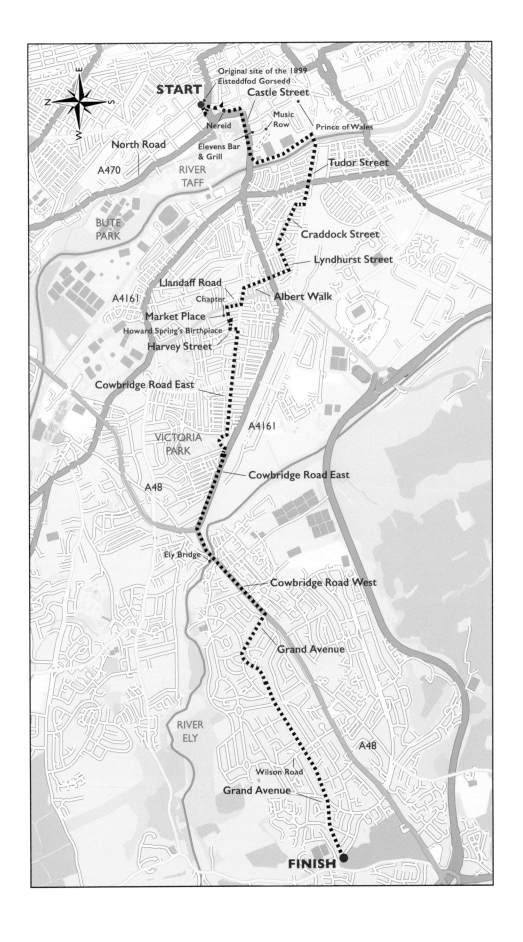

3. THE HEART OF ELY

A walk from the centre of the city to one of its fringes. From the bustling white Portland of the city centre to the red-bricked far reaches of Grand Avenue taking in the Stadium, the straightened river, Taff-tracking Riverside, pub-filled Canton, Victoria Park's water wonderland and the between the wars green glory of Cardiff's pre-eminent western dormitory suburb of Ely.

Start: City Hall
Finish: Grand Avenue
Distance: 5.47 miles
Mostly level with a slow incline towards the end. Return on 13, 17, or 18 bus

www.plotaroute.com/route/487550

Ely isn't on the tourist trail, not normally. But if you want to know Cardiff then seeing this district is vital. I'm walking west from the city's civic centre heading for that place where Ely runs out and Cardiff ends. It's a journey of transition, reminiscent of a Dan O'Neill piece from the *South Wales Echo* of yore, a stride from the centre of the city fathers' power to the place where many of them were born. There's a theory that you can tell from a native Cardiffian's accent on which side of the city they came from. West is where the huge council housing estates came early, in Ely's case between the wars. Here the *ark ark the lark* buzzsaw is strong and the language is littered with *ar right* and *skip*. East, where build was later, the whine is softer and, as few from Llanrumney ever went to sea or worked in the docks *skip* gets replaced by *mate*.

Not that any of this matters at the front of the City Hall. This is a tourist world of Japanese selfie-takers using the clock tower as backdrop and gangs of Spanish kids who sit cross-legged around the fountain on the civic lawn. That fountain has always been a failure. It is supposed to mimic the Prince of Wales' feathers but it only really does this when it's working and today, as with most days, it's not.

South of here stood the Gorsedd stones for the 1899 Eisteddfod. What remains of them now sadly circle a tree in Gorsedd Gardens to the front of the Museum (see p.50). They were moved to enable the construction of Boulevard de Nantes' predecessor, Cathays Park Road, a main highway that connects the two extant portions of the ancient Roman Portway – Newport Road to the east, Cowbridge Road to the west.

My route is through the subway heading south. On the down steps gulls have left trident impressions in the once wet concrete. I emerge to face the art deco Hilton, the old Prudential Building with a new story added. David Nathan's *Nereid*, an execrable sculpture of a sea nymph holding a sea bird stands, generally hated, on a skateboard-protected plinth to my left.

Kingsway bustles. The last remnants of Cardiff's town wall hide on both sides of the road – a few metre stretch as retaining wall for the Council's celebratory flower bed in the Castle moat and a few more as part of the back wall of the Queen Street branch of Santander. Duke Street, which Kingsway becomes, swiftly turns into Castle Street with Gareth Bale's Elevens Bar and Grill on the left. This is the ancient Globe, founded in 1731, and known down the years as The Dukes, the Four Bars Inn and bohemian Dempsey's. Its reinvention as a sports bar and burger & pizza palace perfectly suits the location and the times.

Beyond Womanby Street, Cardiff's Music Row, and Westgate Street, I turn left onto the Millennium Walkway which follows the Taff's now straightened course. The city's graffiti masters once reigned here in an explosion of creative colour but have recently been replaced by the more restrained offerings of Visit Cardiff. This hasn't stopped crews of outgoing Asians having themselves filmed rapping in front of what remains.

The Wood Street bridge onto which this walkway spills rushes away from what was Temperance Town but is today a melee of new high-rise corporate headquarters with the

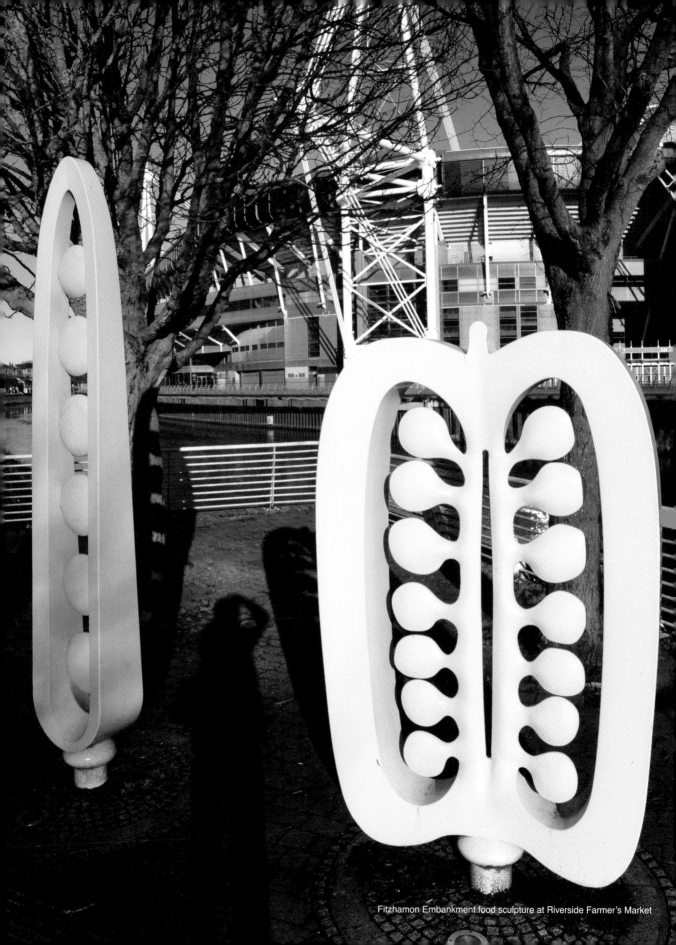

Fitzhamon Embankment food sculpture at Riverside Farmer's Market

BBC at their heart. Looking back along Wood Street the outline of the washed away St Mary Church is clearly visible on the rear wall of Weatherspoon's Prince of Wales. This is an architectural fake rather than an archaeological reality but still more or less in the right place.

West of the bridge is the district of Riverside, the site of the Sunday morning Riverside Farmer's Market with its rock and roll ramble of organic veg stalls, multi-ethnic eateries and suppliers of a diversity of cheese unrivalled anywhere but Harrods. My route zig-zags west through the increasingly mean streets. These are some of the most deprived in the city, places where the sun still shines but only just. In place of driveways and gardens containing pergolas and bay trees in pots Riverside's terraces make do with spaces out front no bigger than sofas. These are regularly stuffed with actual furniture, stained and broken, abandoned to the elements and supplemented by lines of black grey wheelie bins.

On the corner of Smeaton Street I pass Welsh Brewers' Wells Hotel, faded inn sign still swinging but the beer long gone. A local tells me it's flats now but it far more resembles squats. It's in use as an alternative art and music studio with living spaces upstairs. Round the corner there are sprayed pictures of giant bees and multi-coloured orchids. The slogans 'Fascism Must Burn' and 'You Say Austerity We Say Class Warfare' appear in their midst.

I edge north into Canton along Albert Street. Down the years the world here has been thoroughly trashed by the planners to become the mix of affordable housing, back lane and car park it is today. The route I'm taking was originally called Edward Street and once the town's Victorian-era western boundary. Most of what lay beyond was fields. Edward Street was renamed as Albert Street in honour of the Queen's consort. It contained a run of terraced houses from the Duke of York pub on the corner of Wellington Street, passed the Salem Welsh Calvinistic Chapel, right up to the Admiral Napier on Cowbridge Road. At no 32 the novelist and author of *Fame Is the Spur*, Howard Spring, was born in 1889. Spring's family moved to Harvey Street by the Insole Arms around 1895. His birthplace has been exchanged for a contemporary dwelling hardly bigger than the terraced house it replaces. On the wall of Barclays Bank facing the Admiral is a celebratory blue plaque, faded so badly by time and weather as to be totally illegible[7].

The former Insole Arms, Canton

The Corporation, Canton

I am now at that magnificent spot where Leckwith Road and Llandaff Road meet to cross Cowbridge Road East. From here you can touch more pubs than in any other spot in the city. The Corporation, the Canton Cross Vaults, the Plum Tree, the Ivor Davies, the Butcher's Arms, the Canton, plus the bar at Chapter Arts Centre. There were once more. But lucky for Cantonians, as fast as they go they arrive. Saint Canna's Ale House and the Crafty Devil's Cellar are the latest, two microbrewery-powered enlarged front rooms serving great beer to aficionados. The reason for the preponderance of pubs at this spot is historical. Before Chapter Arts Centre was a school it was cattle market. Out of towners needed constant refreshment and the bustle went on all day.

I divert through Harvey Street to look for Howard Spring traces but there are none. The street is a car park with the Insole Arms closed (2014) and redeveloped as a centre for mental health support.

The walk on to Victoria Park passes a mix of shop front and residential garden, as if the road hasn't yet made its mind up which it should be. Victoria Park itself, splendid in the sun, houses the Council's first public waterpark with waterslides,

fountains and watershoots. It's a rival for those at Marbella. As this is high summer the park is brimming. Hard to believe that this was all once Ely Moors, a desperate and unhospitable stretch of wetland and drainage ditch. I stop at the Park View Café opposite, a charity operation run by the church and serving real tea in real cups, far better than anything the city centre's unrecyclable Grande buckets can offer.

Onwards west the districts begin to waver. Canton, Victoria Park and Ely all touch. This is still Cowbridge Road East but with heavier traffic, more grit on the pavements, fewer perambulators, hooded youths on bikes speeding towards you. A poster fixed to a lamppost announces 'Unified Beatz Anti-Social 3rd Birthday Bash powered by Shuddervision Soundsystem'. No mention of venue; those attending will know.

The frontier is ahead. A complex of road and river crossed by multiple bridges. Here Cowbridge Road East meets Cowbridge Road West, the Ely River tumbles south and the main line rail link rolls on towards Swansea. This is Ely's original heartland, home of the Crosswell and Ely breweries, the Chivers pickle and jam factory, the Ely rail station, coal yards, and the paper mill. The mill hangs longest in memory. Cleared now after a hundred and fifty years of rolling paper, its site thoroughly deconsecrated, purified and flattened. I've been walking beside it, unseen to the south, ever since I left the café. It's now a city residential development, part of the Council's plan to house Cardiff's booming population in an 800 home sustainable community that looks in the adverts like a perfect fitted kitchen future but no doubt won't be quite.

Ely does not feel like Canton. This could be an age thing. Ely was constructed between the wars as a place of homes for heroes. These were garden city suburb houses built by Bright and Addicott. Ely was full of grass verge and wide roads. In the fifties and sixties it had a young underemployed population and was the eye of the storm as a probation officer once put it. That eye shifted south to Caerau as time moved and has subsequently sped east to first Pentwyn and now on to the nineties-built brick boxes of new St Mellons.

I finally turn north onto the road of my destination – Grand Avenue. *The* Grand Avenue as the street name plate calls it on the side of the first house. That article, definite and bold, is dropped in all subsequent mentions, right on to the avenue's finish near the city's western boundary. Grand Avenue is long – one and a half miles – and rises almost constantly for its entire length. Its main feature is a central

grass bed, wide enough for two buses to pass. In fact that is what it was designed for. When Grand Avenue was created out of the rolling fields of Red House Farm transport in the new city was still by tram. The proposed Ely tramway would run along the centre of The Grand Avenue, sparking and clanging. It was never built. In 1942 the Council adopted the trolley bus instead and Ely became festooned with overhead wires like much of the rest of the city.

Rounding the half way point, the Wilson Street intersection, I reach the place where Ely's 1991 race riot broke out. This began with an argument about who should be allowed to sell white bread but erupted into a bottle throwing insurrection that ran for three nights and witnessed 175 police facing down 500 rioters. In the past twenty-five years it's not been repeated. Today a quartet of girls sashay the pavement, four abreast and arms linked. Between them they have two iPhones and two sets of earbuds which they share, one ear each. Collectively they sing Ed Sheeran's 'Shape of You' in girl group harmony.

Grand Avenue finishes where it meets the north end of Western Cemetery. This new repository for the dead opened in 1936 as Cathays filled to capacity. It's fittingly shrouded by trees, a peaceful oasis. Beyond are the super stores and multiple shopping parks of the Culverhouse Cross interchange. I sit on a wall and in no time the X1 arrives, the city crossing single decker that gets you there fast. Twenty minutes back to town. Unless, of course, as you are now here you want to explore further. 'Grand Avenue's End to Caerau Hillfort' (see p.77) will do that.

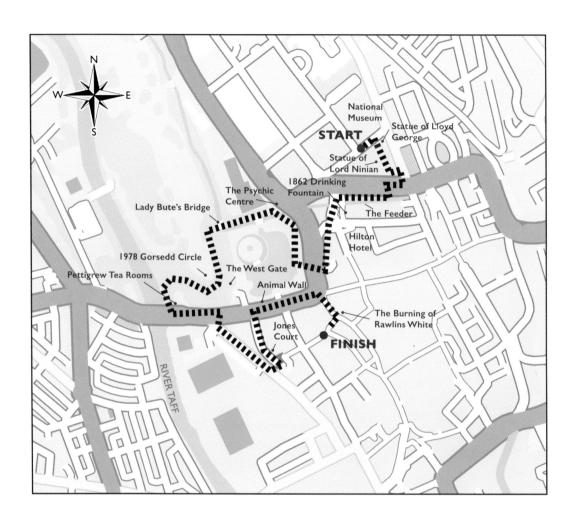

4. A CENTRAL CARDIFF SPIRAL

An easy walk around the City's heart, taking in two Gorsedd Circles, the lost Glamorgan Canal, the Castle, its fakes and follies, the psychic centre, Cardiff's Music Row, and the site of the martyrdom of Rawlins White.

Start: City Hall
Finish: St John's Square
Distance: 1.36 miles
Level

www.plotaroute.com/route/447943

As with the City Hall the steps of the National Museum have the air of Piccadilly about them – millings of people, mostly young, rucksacked and bephoned, and then coaches arriving like cruise liners to deposit more. I'm with John again as we head south on a central Cardiff spiral. Lloyd George gesticulates at us from his plinth, green among the leaves of the linden and the oak at the top end of Gorsedd Gardens. He is so much better in this Michael Rizzello version offering his Welsh Baptist stare of determination at his people, than he is the more recent and soft focus Glynn Williams version in London's Parliament Square. Traces of fossil oyster shell and plant life on the acid rain exposed face of the statue's Portland Stone plinth are clearly visible.

Michael Rizzello's Lloyd George at Gorsedd Gardens

In the park itself, known as Druidical Gardens when it opened in 1909, stands the circle of twelve stone pillars in rough-faced red Radyr breccia. These marked the 1899 visit of the Eisteddfod[8] to Cardiff. Sadly this gateway to another world is no longer what it once was. The central Maen Llog or Logan stone has been removed and surrealistically replaced with a conifer. The inner circle of recumbent slabs in white Penarth alabaster have become so weathered as to be mostly invisible and the taller portal stones that pointed at solstice sunrises have been taken away. If you want to use this place as a time machine then you won't get far.

The gardens offer further statues. Ninian, Bute's son, stands in uniform facing west. South of him, horse mounted, is Lord Tredegar. Bottom end of the park, forever staring at the rumble of traffic along Boulevard de Nantes, is John Cory, just larger than life size, 'coal owner philanthropist'. During the boom times of Victoria and Edward we put up a lot of these things – cast bronze statues of the great and the Cardiff good. As replicas they usually looked much like their subjects. Since then, with the exception of the 1987 bronze Nye Bevan at the end of Queen Street and Lloyd George himself opposite the Museum, we have mostly resorted to blocks of stone, artistically dumb in their uncarved states, or generic figures representing the People – a miner with his lamp, a family group, a crouching child. Until recently, that is. To our poor haul of twentieth century greats we have, at the head of Lloyd George Avenue, now added a lifelike memorial to that other great Cardiffian, Mahatma Ghandi.

We cross the Boulevard to follow the path west along the edge of the 1834 Feeder Canal. This relic of our industrial past was dug to take water from the Taff at Blackweir and deposit it in Bute's brand new West Dock (now filled in) a precursor of Cardiff's greatness to come. Bute reused the medieval mill leat for much of the feeder's track across his parkland but had to excavate anew the section we are following. He insisted later that Cathays Park be protected the new feeder by the planting of a line of trees and installing iron railings. Both still stand.

John talks about his experiences as a professional photographer, often sent to snap subjects who don't turn up or stand about waiting for him in the wrong place. On one occasion, sent to photograph the print maker John Able, he encountered a woman of a certain age, cigarette in mouth, who demanded to know what he was doing with that

Railings alongside the Feeder

camera hanging round his neck. "You want to photograph me?" she asked. For an easy life John obliged only then to be faced with demands from the woman for payment. "You got my picture. You pay me money". The life of the street snapper can be fraught. Able turned up just in time to save John from further hassle.

The Third Marquis of Bute in Friary Gardens

We cross the Feeder bridge at Kingsway, Bute's well-manicured and by act of parliament there for perpetuity Friary Gardens beyond us. His robed statue greens superbly at the park's head. Mayor of Cardiff Alderman Alexander's resited drinking fountain from 1862 has recently been restored, although still fails to function as an actual fountain. Its quotation from the King James Bible on the subject of Jesus and those who drinketh of water failing to deliver.

We turn through the underpass south of the Hilton Hotel. The Hilton, a four star redevelopment of the Prudential Assurance Company regional HQ[9], retains a strong art deco feel. The underpass below Kingsway here, half twentieth century and half nineteenth, once carried the Glamorgan Canal on its route to the sea. The rough sleepers sitting around on the pebble faced towpath remind us in loud voices. "Used to be barges here" shouts one, waving his plastic flagon of Frosty Jack's.

The underpass emerges to face the east wall of Cardiff Castle. The Castle is a either a big fake or an historic survival of some significance. Much depends on your view of history. This was the site of a stone Roman fort which, a thousand years later, the Normans turned into a motte and bailey and then a large stone castle of their own. In subsequent years it was used as a great house, a prison and a farm. Owain Glyndwr sacked it. Town houses clustered against it. When they acquired it (by marriage) the Butes engaged in a complete redevelopment project of unprecedented scale. The architect William Burges was engaged to repair, replace, rebuild and extend. This he did turning the Castle into a nineteenth century Disneyland HQ full of Arab smoking rooms and Gothic revival sword and sorcery banqueting halls with a retelling of Chaucer's tales running across their walls. The Roman sections were carefully preserved and can be seen today at the foot of most of the Castle's outside walls marked by a line of red coloured blocks.

We enter Bute Park, the Castle's grounds, through the gate which faces the Law Courts. Here is Cardiff's much-celebrated Psychic Centre, the meeting place of ley lines, Roman Roads, canals, dock feeders and other traceries of spiritual rule. I've stood here among crowds of visitors and with them felt the shimmering spiritual power. Today, though, in the dull Cardiff damp, nothing sparks. John passes over without a flicker.

Cardiff's West Gate

The path crosses the Feeder ahead via Lady Bute's Bridge. Back in the 1840s Lady Maria, the first wife of the Second Marquis, had this crossing built so she could exit her grand castle apartments to frolic among the greenery of the park itself. Over the years the grounds here have become filled with fakes, phonies and failures. Structures unfinished, the ghosts of what they could have been hovering, counterfeits, false rebuilds. The red box that contained a roped lifebuoy for use in saving unfortunates who fell into the feeder's Taff waters today stands empty. To the south, the refurbished ornamental pond and site of the Castle's medieval mills and tanneries, excavated to much noise and singing a year or so back, has been allowed to become totally overgrown and appears to be on its way to mud-filled oblivion once again. The West Gate and town wall remnant, near the Castle's Herbert Tower are 1920s revisions and not quite in the right place.

Facing the castle is another stone circle. This one, much grander than that in Druidical Gardens, marked the 1978 Eisteddfod visit and was originally sited in Pentwyn. Its central Logan stone, borrowed from the circle in Druidical Gardens, is where you stand to be filled with bardic power. Economics has finally caught up with the present-day Gorsedd's obsession with ceremony and the littering of Wales with latter-day stone circles. Quarried stones have now been replaced with reusable fibreglass replicas. These are moved from site to site year after year. At the southern extremity of the park the wall is topped with stone animals including an ant eater, leopard, seal, bear and a flat tailed beaver. They were designed by Burges in 1866 and ran along the Castle's front. They were moved to their current location following an episode of city street widening after World War 1 and have become one of the city's most enduringly popular attractions.

At their feet among the shrubbery run a line of ferro concrete foundations reminiscent of World War 2 bunkers and gun emplacements. These are the footings for the 4th Marquis's 1930s plan to build a gallery to house his paintings. The war prevented completion and in 1947 the whole estate was donated to the people of Cardiff. What many don't know is that the land in this southern section of Bute Park is actually owned by the Catholic Church. It was given to them by the fifth Marquis as a site for a future cathedral. That never came to pass either.

The River Taff to the west flows safe and sure now that Brunel has stopped its wild course changing by having it channelled and moved to its present cut along the side of what is now the Wales Millennium Stadium. The Taff's 1930s Cardiff Bridge carries the main road west on to Canton and Ely. John and I peer from the river's stone-sided banks at the remnants of an earlier eighteenth century crossing and the present day landing stage for the water taxi. The West Lodge, now renamed after the great Bute gardener as the Pettigrew Tea Rooms provide a welcome stopping place and serve genuinely strong English breakfast tea out of pots and into real cups. A tourist attraction with a real kick.

Westgate Street running from the south side of Castle Street, marks the route along which the Taff formerly flowed. The Town Quay is commemorated with a plaque. Its actual line can be see inside the multi-story where it is delineated by dark coloured brick inserts visible if you get on your knees and stare under the parked cars.

We climb the gentle slope of Quay Street to turn into Womanby Street, or to give it its Danish original name, Houndemanneby, one of the oldest thoroughfares in the city. It is shown on Speed's map of 1610 (Hummanbye Street) and is one of the few places in Cardiff to exhibit a slow medieval curve.

Womanby reeks of age. The restored Jones Court, remnant of Cardiff's slum past, is to our right. The river cobbles of some of the structures are clearly visible. The street is today

Cardiff's music row – site of Clwb Ifor Bach, Bootlegger, Fuel, the Moon and, at its top, along with the now redeveloped Four Bars. A great battle has recently been fought here against apartment and hotel construction. Developers' ability to silence local music by retrospectively claiming the right to remove noise nuisance has been insidious. Recognising the need and economic benefit of filling parts of this now student town with rock and other noisy forms the council finally caved in and instituted a policy to refuse residential developers in favour of music ones. Not, as we pass late afternoon on a bleak Monday, that we can hear a thing.

The walk finishes a short step east along Duke Street, in St John's Square. The turn was once the bane of trolley bus drivers whose poles frequently came off the tracks here. In earlier centuries the square here was much smaller, its north end filled with houses. At its lower end, near St John's Church, one of the oldest of Cardiff structures apart from the Castle, the martyr Rawlins White was allegedly burned to death. This was the price he paid for being the wrong kind of Christian in 1555. In his case Protestant during a time of Catholic revival. Religious intolerance was all the rage in the sixteenth century. Seems like it might be coming back.

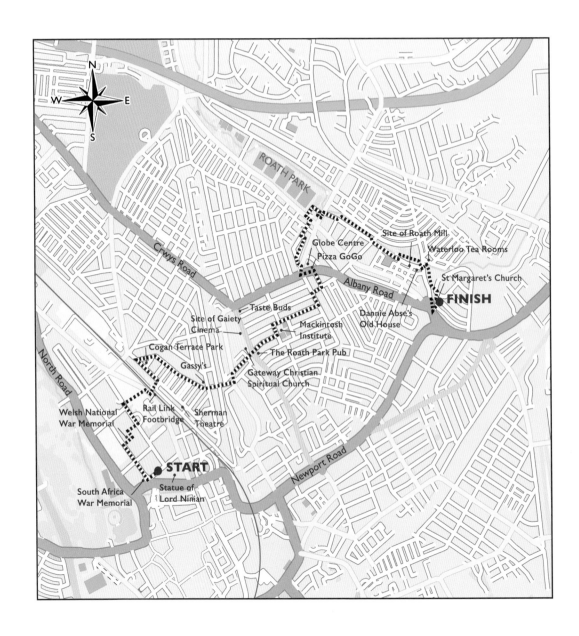

ROATH PARK

Crwys Road

Site of Roath Mill

Globe Centre
Pizza GoGo

Waterloo Tea Rooms

Albany Road

St Margaret's Church

FINISH

North Road

Taste Buds

Site of Gaiety
Cinema

Mackintosh
Institute

Dannie Abse's
Old House

Cogan Terrace Park

The Roath Park Pub

Gassy's

Gateway Christian
Spiritual Church

Welsh National
War Memorial

Rail Link
Footbridge

Sherman
Theatre

Newport Road

START

South Africa
War Memorial

Statue of
Lord Ninian

5. THE REPUBLIC OF ROATH

An easy walk from the Civic Centre through student land Cathays and into the recently bohemian but ancient district of Roath. En route are parks, rivers, churches, a castle, a lost cinema, dystopian futures capes, vanished corn mills and the one-time residences of poets.

Start: City Hall
Finish: St Margaret's Church
Distance: 2.93 miles
Level. Return buses to the centre (too numerous to list) on nearby Newport Road

www.plotaroute.com/route/554719

The classical grandeur of the white Civic Centre with its references to an imperial and almost touchable past is a fitting start for a walk into the Republic of Roath. 'Villa Cardiff' it reads, through the mist, engraved on the City Hall's swaggeringly Baroque façade. In the distance the statue of Lord Ninian, binoculars in hand, peers through increasing murk. We have chosen the foggiest day of the year so far for this ramble.

At the bottom of the red-surfaced King Edward VII Avenue we skirt the South African Memorial from 1908. Peace, a winged angel holds her olive branch, root trailing, up to the gods. This is one of Cardiff's earliest monuments to the war dead. Sculptor Albert Toft's memorial to a now largely forgotten conflict among white men for the heart of black Africa. Welsh names crowd its sides.

Alexandra Gardens, the oasis of manicured calm that separates City Hall from the former Welsh Office, has Ninian Comper's considerably grander circular Welsh National War Memorial at its centre. Rocks marking the dead of further conflicts as well as a number of other apparently randomly chosen causes dot the remainder of the park. John takes numerous pics, most to emerge doused in misty grey. He'll need to return when it is bright.

We pass the early University College Building on Museum Avenue with its engraved gateposts reading 'OVT' rather than 'OUT'. As Latin used no letter U neither did our Edwardian seats of learning. Further on is what for decades was an empty lot known as the Ranch. Today it is crowded

Welsh National War Memorial, Alexandra Gardens

with the University's flourishing. High density post-war towers and concrete fronted accommodations cluster together. They use every last inch of space. We walk between them, following the line of College Road, and emerge on Park Place. Here we are faced with the University's latest development. An unprecedented run of Park Place buildings, including the existing Students Union, are being demolished to create a new age future powered Centre for Student Life. Work no doubt completed by the time you read this. Education in Cardiff is as big as coal once was.

The footbridge now in front of us crosses the main Merthyr and Aberdare Valley rail link north. This runs through the city to squeeze by Caerphilly Mountain and reach into the vast hinterland beyond. I suggested in *Real Cardiff The Flourishing City* that the only way of properly uniting the capital with its dependent territories might be to flatten that mountain so we could all see each other. Hasn't happened yet.

The bridge at Cathays Station

As it's 8.30 in the morning rail traffic is heavy and scores of travellers bound for the both the University and the Civic Centre are exiting onto Cathays Station and pouring over the footbridge. John, who occasionally finds himself happier shooting people than he is landscape, channels Henri Cartier-Bresson to make the best of this decisive moment.

As a district, early Cathays was almost entirely workers' housing. Tight no-bathroomed terraces built within walking distance of places of work. Along the railway there were many: the waggon works of the Taff Vale Railway, coal yards, engine sheds, brickworks, patent fuel manufacturers who pressed small coal into usable briquettes. All gone now.

We are on Senghenydd Road, famous for its radical mosques, its Sherman Theatre and its department of continuing education, home for a generation of French learners, history buffs, philosophers and other escapees from philistine life. We pass Cogan Terrace Park, a triangular scrap of green, dismal compared to the Cathays Park glories we have just departed, to walk along Miskin Street. The area has almost entirely been given over to student accommodation. Here you live clustered, kitchens with sour milk and your beans always eaten by others, front room beat boxes playing till dawn. It's cheaper and much more sociable than the box flats of the Ikea-like Purpose Built Student Accommodation (PBSA) towers springing up elsewhere across the city.

Miskin Street soon hits Salisbury Road at Gassy's, the weakly renamed student drinkery that for years was known as the far more memorable Gassy Jacks. Here all-day all giant breakfast diners and convenience food stores supply an ever-changing population. We track down Lowther Road passing under the rail link north to Caerphilly. On the walls beside us are the soon-to-be-removed remains of photographer Dan Green's Uganda art work. Black faces from Tororo worn down by Cardiff graffiti and Cardiff rain.

This is the boundary. Behind us lies Cathays. In front is Roath – the place that Cardiff was almost named after, but that's a different story[10].

Northcote Street takes us past Gateway Christian Spiritualist Church – 'Letterbox in lane entrance. Spiritual healing every Tuesday morning'. Northcote Street Lane, to the spiritualist's left, is an unreconstructed relic of worn-by-poverty city past. Garage doors and broken walls tumble at each other, woodwork worn to splinters, black pointing loose and lost and the whole frontage spray-painted to oblivion by successive waves of street artists. In sunlight this place is a multi-coloured vibrant dystopia, except today there is no sun. It's worth a diversion although, as a result of new build[11], in action as I write, access at the end to City Road via the soon-to-be-demolished twin-domed Gaiety Cinema is now blocked. The only route is back to hit City Road at the Northcote Street junction.

Northcote Street Lane

A second diversion worth managing, and one John and I take, is to head left a hundred yards or so to find Taste Buds, a café selling builders tea in giant mugs and old fashioned white bread toast swimming with butter. Like they used to do it. We sit in the steamy warmth, a radio playing loudly in the background. Locals around us are eating great plates of pie, beans and ketchup covered chips. You can easily get out of here with change from £5.

Taste Buds, City Road

City Road, in my youth a street of car salesrooms, is now one of the most multi-cultural thoroughfares in the city. The population is as transient as they come, a home to recent Cardiff arrivals from the Middle East, Asia and Africa. It's now known as Arabic Street by many of its users but was originally a muddy track called Plwca Lane. Its name was changed to Castle Road in 1874 as the landowner developed what was once rough farmland to build a great house, Plas Newydd, in its centre. The name changed again in 1905 when Cardiff's status was elevated to city.

We turn into Kincraig Street at the Roath Park. This labyrinthine public house opened in 1886 as The Castle and in a long and varied history among other things launched poetry adventurers Cabaret 246 in the 1980s and was campaign office for the Roatherendum[12] in 2014. For those wondering why this district is known as The Republic of Roath this is where the vote was cast. 800 for and 2 against independence. Local politicians Sir Alfred Street and Dr Glen Roy told me that "We can now have our bananas any shape we want."

Kincraig leads down to the Mackintosh Institute, home of a whole raft of sporting activities as well as regular craft fairs (or possibly fayres) and the Saturday Roath Farmer's Market. When it was built this mansion was known as Plas Newydd (new place), a name later revived by the Council for electoral ward purposes. When castellations were added in the 1830s it became known as Roath Castle. Ownership eventually shifted to the splendidly named Alfred Donald Mackintosh, the Mackintosh of Mackintosh, who gave many of the streets developed on his land Scottish names. In 1891 the grounds and house were donated for the benefit of residents of the Mackintosh estate. It still serves that purpose today.

Southwards lies Claude Road Lane and beyond it red-fronted Pizza GoGo, site of Ffynon Bren, one of the three great Penylan Holy Wells. When I called in and asked if the curative waters still rose in their back garden I was met with blank stares[13].

We loop through the Globe Centre courtyard. This was the site of the Penylan (later Globe) Cinema which showed continental films in true fleapit style from 1910 to 1985. The route crosses Wellfield Road to go down Bangor Street and on to find Penylan Library and Community Centre on the corner of Roath Park Recreation ground. The community centre is a huge advance on the ragged brick library and windowless blockhouse changing rooms that stood here in the 1950s. Outside Roath youth still spark and shine. They do wheelies and timewasting in a rush of growing much as they have done on this corner since the park was created.

Roath Park Rec, a significant green expanse and home to countless football and baseball matches, was where Santa once arrived by helicopter and Buffalo Bill brought his horse mounted Indians to whoop and charge to the star-struck delight of local children. The flat and featureless sward was crossed by the errant Nant y Lleucu, the Roath Brook, but that has now been hard channelled along the park's eastern extreme. In 1887 the land was filled with tip refuse to level the stream's original course. By the turn of the century the whole lot was surrounded by iron railings but those have long disappeared.

We cross Penylan Hill to follow Sandringham Road alongside the site of nineteenth century brickworks and what has now become known as Roath Brook Gardens. Here the Save Our Trees campaign fought a lengthy battle against National Resources Wales over just how much environmental damage and tree felling would end up being carried out in the pursuit of flood defence. The flood works themselves with their new revetments, intrusive flood barriers, and river diversions, have changed this Edwardian parkscape forever.

Roath Brook Gardens

Roath Mill Gardens further south was once a mill pond serving the thousand year old Roath Mill. That structure and a few attendant cottages, among the oldest mentioned in extant Cardiff records, were demolished in 1897. Rubin Eynon's sculptured model replica stands on the site. The millers are buried at St Margaret's Church. The stream, which flowed along what is now Marlborough Road was diverted to provide the mill race.

In Waterloo Gardens (all the streets around here are named after battles – Agincourt, Alma, Trafalgar) the peaceful lawns and cherry trees have been replanted and surrounded by a bending maze of flood defence walls and banks. Centrepiece is a heavy-handed structure half-summerhouse, half-trellis and succeeding as neither. It's neat enough but not what people remember. As a boy the poet Dannie Abse carved his name in the hut, now demolished. I went to see it before that happened but couldn't find a trace. Dannie lived at 66 Sandringham Road for a time and there's a Rhys Davies Trust plaque on the front to celebrate.

South of the park is our destination, St Margaret's Church, centre of old Roath. Stand in the churchyard which still shows some of its circular origins in the way its walls bend and you can see a whole village. Church, green (the round-about), great house (Roath Court, now a funeral home), the site of the smithy (on the Newport Road junction), the mill, the farm (Ty Mawr, end of Southminster Road). A scattering of cottages ran up Albany.

The present neo-Gothic St Margaret's, designed by John Pritchard, was developed on the site of an earlier whitewashed country church in the 1860s. That simple building had been extended to include a magnificent mausoleum for the Butes in 1800. The whole thing is built on a mound which makes you think that maybe this was once an iron age fort. In 1869 the Marquis of Bute who was funding the new church project converted to Catholicism. Payments ceased and the proposed spire was truncated as a tower.

Inside the window which lets holy light into the catafalque-filled mausoleum was one that originally graced earlier country church. Pieces of lintel have also been reused as gate pillar tops on the St Margaret's Crescent entrance. The mausoleum holds nine Bute bodies in triple coffins, pitch-sealed, and contained within massive red Peterhead polished granite tombs. Their style imitates that of the Tsars in St Petersburg.

We're done and it is at this point the fog decides to lift. Sheaves of sunlight come flooding through the trees and the whole landscape shines.

Excellent tea can be had at the Waterloo Tea Rooms opposite the park and there's an overkill of buses (44, 45, 49, 50, X3, X5, X45, X11) passing along nearby Newport Road to take you back to the centre. Or in John's case Newport – Wales' First City – the first one you get to when arriving from England, that is.

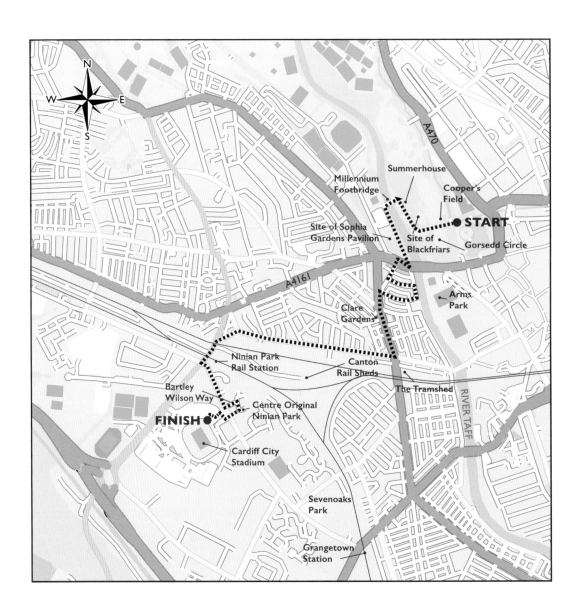

6. THE NEW NINIAN PARK

An urban walk from green space to green space moving south west through the city's less-travelled Riverside. This route starts in Cooper's Field, just north of the Castle, and ends at Cardiff football's focal point. Easy travelling along non-tourist streets with plenty of refreshments and shopping at the Cardiff City stadium end.

Start: Cooper's Fields, Bute Park
Finish: Cardiff City Stadium
Distance: 2.28 miles
Level. Return to Cardiff Centre by train from either Grange-town or Ninian Park stations

www.plotaroute.com/route/447961

Cooper's Fields haven't seen any actual coopers in a long time. This is the section of Bute Park west of the feeder that is used these days less as a green open space and more a site for whatever show the Council currently needs to promote. The Champions League hospitality pavilions, the RHS Flower Show, the Cardiff Rathayatra Festival of Chariots, the Euro 2016 Fanzone, Florence + the Machine performing at the Big Weekend, the LGBT Mardi Gras and the Round Table firework display have all been there in recent times. It's the only public park I've discovered to have its own dedicated entry on Ticketline.

The land was once part of the sliding Taff's river bed and has done its time as pasture for Blackfriars Farm and the Marquis of Bute's deer park. During the Second World War it grew veg. But today it's calm, green-grassed, full of summer tourists eating ice creams and with the Castle as backdrop.

I pass the Gorsedd circle again (see p.54) and its impressive central altar stone, in use, as ever, as a base for picnicking families, skirt the revitalised remains of the Blackfriars monastery with its graves and air of municipal antiquity, to head north along the river towards the Summerhouse Café. The path runs beside the park's great herbaceous border, that part of the city centre's green lung that still looks like the 1950s. It was created sixty years ago by Director of Parks Bill Nelmes[14] who made it long and deep and with enough over the top flowering variety to be the envy of every great house in Wales.

Beside the café is the still new (to Cardiffians) Millennium Footbridge which I cross to reach the Taff's west bank bund. In the days of rock and roll and the annual Ideal Home Exhibition, it would have deposited me right behind Sophia Gardens Pavilion. That piece of Cardiff's musical past where everyone from Bill Haley to Jimi Hendrix played to swooning crowds disappeared in 1983. The Pavilion was a great Cardiff public hall erected in 1951 in the teeth of the post-War recession. Its look was that of a miniature South Bank Festival Hall, 50s concrete, brick and glass, but built on the cheap. Challenging budgets were met by reusing a hanger transported from Stormy Down aerodrome and filling it with stacking chairs. The heavy snows of 1981-82 collapsed the roof and demolition soon followed. It is currently a car park and National Welsh bus station. Its origins as a flower-bed and fountain-enhanced public park for the poor of industrial Cardiff have been long forgotten.

Sophia Gardens was an 1854 good work carried out by Lady Sophia Rawdon-Hastings, the wife of the second Marquis of Bute. It had a bandstand, fountain, bowling green, clubhouse and lake and was a great addition to the booming coal port although, it has to be said, not entirely an altruistic creation. It was more compensation for the closure by the Butes for private use of the previously publicly accessible Castle Grounds.

South of the Park, skirting the edge of the Taff's Cardiff Bridge I enter the district of Riverside to walk down Victorian Green Street and then zig-zag along Mark Street,

Brook Street and Coldstream Terrace. Here the houses have an unexpected seaside B&B feel with front windows displaying collections of garden gnomes, tea pots and ceramic yachts. One has a plywood cut out map of the British Isles emblazoned with the resolute tract 'As for me and my house we will serve the Lord'. Brook Street bends like a river tributary, which it may well once have been. The lost River Canna curving down from its Llandaff Fields origins to enter the now flood-barriered Taff.

Coldstream Terrace, Riverside

Over the river is the Arms Park, what's left of it, wrapped around the back of the interstellar space ship that is the Millennium Stadium. Overlooking them are the clad walls of the Holiday Inn. In the days when this was the Crest Hotel, Australia's leading poet, Queen's Gold medal winner Les Murray and author of *Schindler's Ark*, novelist Thomas Keneally, headlined the Cardiff Literature Festival here. They read to a large and enthusiastic audience. When done Murray went off with the lads for a curry in Bridge Street. Keneally was taken to a silver service dinner at the Park.

On Brook Street, beyond the curved apartment rebuild of the Millers Tavern (the earlier Coldstream) we are, if road names are anything to go by, in ancient Norman territory – Clare Gardens, Dispenser Gardens – inner city green spaces with their swings and play areas, abandoned park keeper's hut, locked and rotting. These days Riverside is a focus for the city's ethnic minorities. Halal food stores, places offering phone cards that get you cheap connection to Pakistan. 'Eid Special Offer Sheep £2.99 Boal Fish £7.99' reads one handmade window sign.

Clare Street, which I've been walking, turns right here into the final stretch of Tudor Road. To the south under the main rail line is the Tramshed. This was the Grangetown depot for Cardiff's trams (and later trolley buses), a repair and maintenance centre of some size. Its red brick gables, all eleven of them, each with two high level semi-circular windows are distinctive. The structure was Grade Two listed in 1997. It's been given new age wings now as a 1000 capacity music venue and arts centre. Tinariwen have played along with UB40, Public Enemy and The Charlatans. This week it's Eliza Carthy and Scouting For Girls.

But I'm heading west to where the trainspotters' paradise of Canton Sheds stood. Tudor Road gives way here to

Ninian Park Road with an array of great engineers celebrated in the streets leading off: Telford, Stephenson, Brunel, Trevithick, Smeaton. Canton steam rail sheds were built in 1882 on a rambling site next to the main rail line as the Great Western's Welsh engineering base. After nationalisation they continued as a heavy overhaul depot for British Rail's steam stock. 86c, as Canton engines were coded, was a designation to watch. Back then trainspotters could cross the line on the footbridge, pad in hand, and wander more or less where they liked. Today the site is a major diesel locomotive traction maintenance depot and guarded by fence, CCTV and key padded gate with the resolute thoroughness of a military base. Come here spotting and you won't see a thing.

Eldon Street, as Ninian Park Road was first known, went past the Electricity Works before joining Leckwith Road and plunging south under the rail link's two bridges. Today those works are an industrial estate with the Crafty Devil Brewing Company as its centrepiece. South of the tracks and beyond Ninian Park Station the atmosphere changes. Gone are the close streets, the Victorian darkness, the grit and grime of inner city, to be replaced by space and light, the green parkland of Jubilee Rec with the new football stadium beyond.

Cardiff City followers will know this place and recognise its resonance. The site of Ninian Park football ground now clustered with Redrow houses, the preserved blue gates, the departed celebrated in their memorial garden, the huge car parks, owner Vincent Tan's new and as yet unsullied stadium glistening in their centre. This is the home of City victoriousness to come. We are waiting. Sam the man is a memory. Manager Neil Warnock now steers the ship.

I divert into the centre of the Ninian Park housing development with its winding Bartley Wilson Way. Wilson was the clubfooted, Bristol-born founder of Riverside AFC in 1899. That's the team that first played at Sophia Gardens, got themselves adopted by the town as the official side in 1908, and transferred to the brand new Ninian Park ground in 1910. By this time they'd changed their name to Cardiff City AFC and set about conquering all. The Sloper Road grounds became Ninian Park, named after Lieutenant-Colonel Lord Ninian Crichton-Stuart, the second son of the third Marquis of Bute and MP for Cardiff. He was killed at the Battle of Loos in 1915.

Bartley Wilson Way rounds towards the estate's core where a metal plaque has been set in the ground marking the kick off centre of the original pitch. Forever celebrated. I stand next to it and look out through the estate's gates over Sloper Road to the new stadium beyond. Out front is a statue of Fred Keenor, cup in arm. Keenor was the Bluebirds' greatest player leading the team to FA Cup success in 1927. That victory is almost a hundred years ago now and they still talk about it.

On a non-match day Cardiff City Stadium stands isolated in the winds. Only a few cars dot its vast carparks. The skies are big above them. These were once the Leckwith Moors, badly drained wastelands of mud and damp. The nearby brickworks have been built over as Cardiff's bus depot. The Grange tannery next door has vanished. The rest is smattered with council housing and big box stores.

If football and the Bluebirds' ethos fails to thrill then divert to one of the nearby branches of Marks & Spencer's, Lidl, Next, Asda or the other many wonders of the Capitol Shopping Park, an essential funding-backdrop to the new Stadium's 2014 construction. Better, and standing right next to the Stadium's red-seated Ninian Stand, are the copious splendours of Glamorgan Archives with free access to all the local history anyone could ever want.

The easy route back to the city is to catch a train on the City Line from Ninian Park Station but I choose instead to walk the 15 minutes south along Sloper Road's full length. At Grangetown Station I catch a TfW Sprinter from Penarth to emerge at Cardiff Central on a newly built platform, somehow without a ticket. Cardiff Central is changing, flexing out like the inside of Dr Who's Tardis. The planners are turning it into a leisure and shopping destination. I have to queue at the unpaid fares desk, knowing more now about the western city than I once did.

Beyond the barrier I find myself in a Central Square so new and rebuilt that I'm momentarily lost, dumbfounded by the rush of towering structures that lap in at me where the bus station once was and where Temperance Town lolled a century back. But then, in the distance, familiar St Mary Street reasserts itself. I've been two and a half hours without a stop but a hundred cafés, coffee shops, restaurants, bars, diners and every other sort of eatery imaginable lie ahead. In the twentieth first century it's what this city does best.

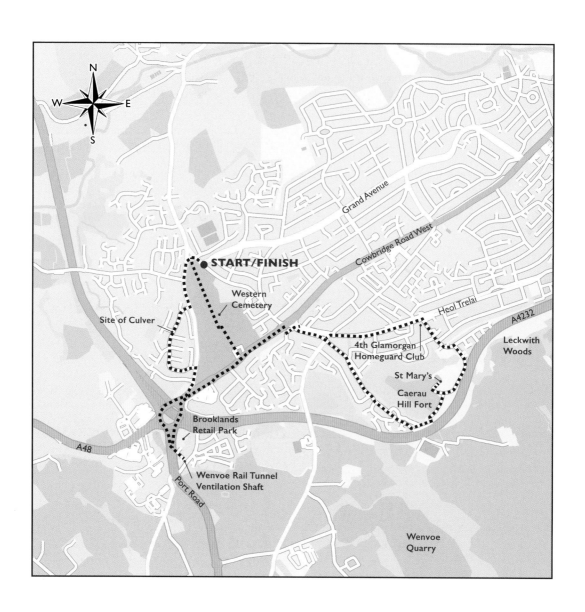

7. GRAND AVENUE'S END TO CAERAU HILLFORT

A circular walk right on Cardiff's Western Fringe. From Ely's Grand Avenue terminus to the site of the Culver House, a detour through retail heaven to view the well-hidden ventilation shaft for the now abandoned Wenvoe rail tunnel, a hike through the western city's post second World War housing estate of Caerau, an unexpected climb through woodland to reach the ramparts of an iron age fort and the ruined remains of St Mary's Church. Finally, a traverse of Western Cemetery and the Commonwealth War Graves to meet Grand Avenue once more in all its dual carriage grass islanded splendour.

Start: Grand Avenue
Finish: Grand Avenue
Distance: 4.60 miles
A circular walk, mostly level with a steep but short clamber on to the hillfort. Return buses to centre: 13, 17 & 18

www.plotaroute.com/route/485822

I reach the edge. Ely doesn't quite end here although it might feel like it. I've come up on the bus from the far east of the city to alight just before the shopping trolley and car-filled tangle of the Culverhouse Cross retail parks. Culverhouse is a Cardiff gateway. It's where the city finishes and the Vale of Glamorgan begins. The roads, and there are many, intertwine at a huge multi-level junction, a mirror of the Coryton Gyratory to the north, but smaller – just.

A culverhouse is a dovecote, a grand pigeon shed from an era when the birds were kept for food rather than racing. The one this junction is named after, Culver House, was an ancient farm that lasted until the early 1960s when its lands were redeveloped for housing. The Michaelston Estate, as the development is named, squashes between the Ely link road, the A4232, and the Cemetery. It is a territory of well-tended gardens, a house gate guarded by two miniature sphinxes, a recently closed pub (The Michaelston), no road humps. Culver House stood right at road centre where Panteg Close joins Llanover Road. It is uncelebrated. Even the pub named after it, The Culverhouse, on Cowbridge Road West, has now changed its name to Coopers Carvery. The past vanishes through our fingers.

The gates to Western Cemetery, Grand Avenue, Ely

I steer south through the estate to emerge at the edge of the monster junction. Boards offer directions to each of the five retail parks. To visit them all would be a driving challenge but for walkers it's a snip. Facing down the Vale's intrusion up Port Road a badly maintained sign announces the start of Cardiff, the nation's capital. The name of Baltimore, a once twinned but now, for no good reason I can discern, unceremoniously untwinned city, can be seen hovering just above those that still formally share their names with us. After being twinned with Stuttgart in 1955, Cardiff adopted Lugansk in the Ukraine in 1958, followed that with Nantes in 1964, and then Xiamen, China, in 1983 and finally (although who is to say what the future might hold) Hordaland, Norway, in 1996.

The equivalent sign, welcoming all to the Vale, announces bilingually that this is the home of the National Eisteddfod 2012. A thing to look forward to.

In the Brooklands retail park (Pizza Hut, Aldi, Curry's/PC World, Burger King) is an outpost of orange sunburst B&M home stores. Secured behind vandal-proof fencing to its rear is a barb-wire topped breeze blockhouse with a notice that reads 'DANGER DEEP HOLE'. This is the abandoned ventilation shaft to the disused Wenvoe rail tunnel[15] beneath. Cardiff subterraneans marvel over the continued existence of this edifice, dreaming perhaps that someday the tunnel will reopen, reinvented as a pedestrian adventure or a cycleway. Who knows?

Blockhouse protecting Wenvoe rail tunnel ventilation shaft

I need now to get from here to the southern greenness of the Caerau housing estate by the most direct route. I choose a track which skirts the Brooklands housing development (formerly the Cambrian caravan park) to the retail park's south. This peters out in dense wood after a few hundred metres and I find myself tangled in a mix of thick blackthorn and all-enveloping blackberry bramble on a trail that would be called a sheep track if it were in rural country.

This illegal and trespassing passage of mine ignores health and safety completely and stumbles along the top of the Ely Link road's cutting to eventually meet the ramparts of Caerau Lane Bridge. Here I find myself finally unsnagged and blissfully free on the rim of southern Caerau. It's been an ill-advised diversion and one I don't recommend readers repeating. The safer route is clearly back along the pavement to Cowbridge Road West, past the site of the onetime earth moving giants Caterpillar (now Tool Store) to run parallel to an area known in earlier times as Saint's Well. The well had healing qualities but is now lost, let into the sewers, the fate of many of Cardiff's sources of spiritual power. The name Saintswell has become Cymrified in the splendid mangle and rather rude sounding nonsense of Cyntwell. But we won't dwell. Let's move on.

Caerau proper is entered via Heol Trelai. This is the southern equivalent of Ely's Grand Avenue but lacking that thoroughfare's green central reserve and, dare I say it, sense

of grandeur. Nonetheless it is green and wide and, today, full of light. The walk is downhill towards Cwrt yr Ala Road. Looking like a suburban street this follows the line of an ancient track running below Caerau Wood. Here the isolation hospital has been redeveloped for housing by Barrett. At the end is a lane which climbs Spillers Hill. This is the hillfort access, one of them.

Hillforts and their racial memory have followed a good many poets around for centuries. There is something about sites of earth mystery and the wilfully misunderstood theology that emanates from them, that catches the soul and pours on out though the pen. If as a poet you still use a pen. I've spotted increasing numbers turning up at readings with no more than a few dictated lines read out from the screen of their phones. Gone are the days of hefty notebooks and crackling plastic carriers full of early drafts, mostly in the wrong order and inevitably spilled over the floor before the attendant crowd. All part of the experience if not the act. The era has changed, the form has moved on.

Chris Torrance, bard of Pontneddfechan and master of the poetic ley, was one of my introductions to these lost sources of spiritual energy. The other was John Michell with his heretical reinvention of earth mystery and tracking of the sources of antique power[16]. I get a sense of this 40 year old personal history rising again as I breach the densely wooded slope to emerge in the wide green meadow centre of the hillfort known now as Caerau.

That such an ancient place, source of tribal authority, centre of leys and a mystic portal should exist so close to the Welsh capital's centre and right on the edge of one of the city's largest and often rumbustious housing estates is amazing. It should be wrecked but how do you vandalise a hill? Lucky for Caerau there are no through routes, like as those at Avebury, nor buildings beyond a single ruined church. St Mary's. And that structure adds to the mystery much as roofless St Michael's tower does atop Glastonbury Tor.

The hillfort forms part of the great British prehistory before the arrival of the Romans when the ancients held sway and the druids ran the world. Around here the dominant tribe (and fearsome Roman resisters) were the Silures. Swarthy, short, with black curly hair. Looking a lot like the Iberians or the Gauls, suggested the Roman bureaucrat Jordanes. If you check the locals in the nearby branch of Lidl you'd guess that some of the original inhabitants still remain.

Hillforts were palisaded enclosures often with outer ditches and ramparts. They were constructed on defensible land with viewpoints overlooking all possible avenues of attack. The ramparts protected a village of roundhouses and other structures, space for animals, food stores, metal workers, water supply. Being made of wood none of this stuff has survived. In fact, to the trained eye neither have the foundations or the inevitable marks residential occupation leaves on the land.

Time Team have been to this one. They came in 2012. More recently there has been an extensive local Caer heritage project which has published a series of explanatory leaflets and trails and has great plans for the future. Through archaeological research the project has uncovered significant Roman and Iron Age remains as well as evidence of a ringwork on the north eastern corner. In medieval times there was also a castle here.

Ruined St Mary's Church (built in the 13th century, circular graveyard, deconsecrated in the 1960s) has been tidied since I last visited. That was in 2003 in the company of the green-bearded guitarist and Bard of Ely, Steve Andrews. Back then there was smashed glass, splintered wood and much evidence of drink and drug use. Today it's more as Torrance might enjoy, pastoral, mystical and timeless.

St Mary's Church and earthworks

I descend using the gentler route down Church Lane through the fields of the now built-on Church House Farm. I pass the end of Hillfort Close where the West End Brickworks stood and join roaring (by comparison) Heol Trelai again. At the junction is the 4th Glamorgan Homeguard Club advertising Carling Extra Cold and Coors Light. According to Police records supplemented by the evidence of a burned out caravan in the car park this is an anti-social behaviour hotspot. But it's as peaceful as the Sarsaparilla Shop today.

My track back returns me up Heol Trelai with half the street sign, the *Heol* component, missing. I pass again through the enchanting Cyntwell along Cowbridge Road West to the gates of Western Cemetery. Unlike Cathays with its wonderland of heart shaped curving pathways, tall trees and lack of signboarding, Western is grid patterned and open. With its Jewish, Muslim and Greek sections it reflects the changing nature of the city. The Jews place small pebbles on the gravestones, never flowers. Many locals go in for sentimental verse engraved on marble slabs and, increasingly, photographs of the deceased. Once austere and inevitably Christian the world of death is changing rapidly.

In the far western corner are the Commonwealth War Graves, 30 in a serried white stoned plot here and a further 120 scattered throughout the cemetery. Behind them are the memorial stones recalling the last resting places of other service personnel in graves which can no longer be maintained in the churchyards where they were laid to rest. Beyond are trees which fail to completely shut out the sound of Culverhouse traffic.

At the top end of the cemetery where Grand Avenue ends and the bus back to the city centre can be caught the road sign is a mirror of the one on Heol Trelai. Here, though, the word *Avenue* has not been removed but instead obliterated in three different colours – black, purple and marker scribble. Someone is trying to tell us something but I've no idea what it is.

MN

T. C. BROCK
DONKEYMAN
S.S. "PORT JACKSON"
6TH APRIL 1944

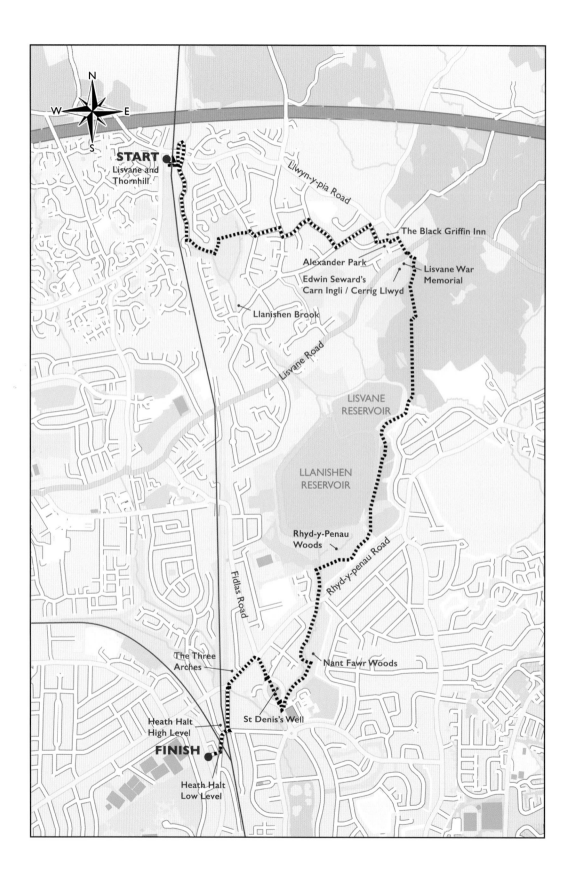

8. LISVANE TO HEATH HALT

A slowly rolling downhill walk through Lisvane at the edge of the city to the High and Low Level railway halts in the centre of the Heath. En route we cross fields, follow streams and penetrate woodland. We track reservoirs and discover holy wells. Start and finish on the train but as ever in the city there are always buses.

Start: Lisvane & Thornhill Rail Station
Finish: at Heath Halt
Distance: 3.99 miles
Return to Cardiff City Centre can be made by train, the 86 bus on Heath Park Avenue just up from the stations, or Nextbike, liberated from the stand on Lake Road North outside

www.plotaroute.com/route/607017

This being a bank holiday the car park at Lisvane & Thornhill rail station is largely bereft of cars. On a week-day it would be the reverse as the local population transports itself to its work, shop, and study destinations. You don't walk much in Llys-Faen, in this leafy place where the pavements often falter there are few places to stroll to. Lisvane, Llys-faen, stone court, origin lost in the mists, the courthouse faded from memory, had a population of 207 in the mid nineteenth century. Most of it didn't exist when I was a kid and being well to do was a rarity. But in the new Lisvane of detached houses and sweeping drives all that has changed.

Crossing the district through a wavering diagonal of streets I've never visited is a revelation. The place is new crisp brick perfection. Rarely a shrub unpruned, no mismatched repairs, no hanging gutters, no streaks of rain-drip mould nor stains of age cross the ever white walls. But if you live here where do you go? What do you do? There's a background hum of motorised grass cutters and thrumming leaf blowers. You do that. Garden. Admire the view. Enjoy the sun. Simmer and slump.

We snake past the bold Lego townhouses of Clos Llysfaen, one called Railway Cuttings with actual Lego in a front window. Behind are the train tracks, in front the as yet unadopted Clos unencumbered by litter. High Merc count. No-one out washing the things yet.

There's a gate on the left giving access to ancient woodland, how it was for centuries in these parts until the population boomed and the house builders came. Coed-y-Felin (Mill Wood) is the new name, a recalling of the mill that stood at the southern end until as recently as 1962. These things exist for century on century and are then overnight flattened, on a whim it seems, to provide space for a residence that might make the developer a few thousand today but leaves a yawning gap in history. Of the hundreds we once had how many remain in Cardiff today? Two or three. If that.

In contrast to the road the Coed-y-Felin woodlands are fully Council adopted and supported by an active group of Friends. You can tell by their almost manicured nature. There are trails, stepped paths, sleeper bridges, round stones to cross the brook (it's the Nant Fawr, the Roath Brook again, this far north and still rushing), tree stumps carved into eruptions of the Green Man with his bearded woodland face. No chucked cans, discarded hardcore, splashed graffiti, broken benches, no gangs of youth idling in the verdant clear.

But it's a brief crossing. We emerge, calmness injected, peace upon us, onto Heol Cefn On, the ridge of ash trees with one 'n' gone. There's a porticoed house here splendidly known as The Hazards. On the drive of another stands a black open top with the number plate BR16GSY, the one John would have if he ever got to own a supercar. Among

Nant Fawr stepping stones at Coed-y-Felin, Lisvane

these new structures front gardens lack walls, the private and public realms merging, as if this were American suburban sprawl rolled out beyond the money-making city.

The roads join and cross. Millwood. Mill Road. Larch Grove. Rosewood Close. Rowan Way. Developers' names. A detour down Mill Road gets a glimpse of the house designed as his own residence by the great Cardiff architect of the heroic period, Edwin Seward. Seward built the Coal Exchange, Cardiff Infirmary, the Morgan Arcade, the Insole Court North Wing. With Lisvane House he created a great Arts and Crafts confection, as big as six houses (which it has today been divided into). He didn't stay there long, however. When his plans for a great new Cardiff Civic Centre, his "Dream of the future", with a People's Palace on Cathays Park, were rejected, he left for Dorset, turning his back on the Welsh capital's white Portland Stone.

In eastern Lisvane, where the district runs out and farmland temporarily returns, lies the old hamlet core. The Memorial Hall advertising a forthcoming plant sale and yoga lessons, the pub, the church, the blacksmiths. The smithy is naturally no longer but the other two still remain.

The tiny Alexander Gardens here has a 'No Ball Games' sign in its long-grassed approach. On the fence is another reminding everyone that the park is for the quiet enjoyment of residents only and that the nearest casualty department is located at University Hospital, Cardiff. A stubby run of semis with gas meters in white mildewed boxes on their outside walls stand nearby. A lane pitches us into the Black Griffin car park opposite St Denis' Church, slate saddle-back roofed tower, fourteenth century origins but clearly built and rebuilt many times since then. Next to the store and the hair studio and the obligatory estate agents is a flattened space with a sign offering a forthcoming selection of new two bed properties. The locals cannot wait.

Beside the war memorial and the new mini roundabout, trafficked now by cars too large for the lanes and giant cross-country SUVs that ought to be in the fields rather than blocking the meagre tarmac, stands a great stone house with the word JET in a diamond plaque high on its gable end. Rather than a mansion this is actually a semi with one half known as Carn Ingli and the other as Cerrig Llwyd. It was built by JET, Cardiff builder par excellence, J.E. Turner, in 1931.

We cross the stile on Maerdy Lane just behind the War Memorial. Carmageddon instantly turns to pastoral purity. Fields roll into the distance, motorways are invisible, buildings are gone. We could be in rural Carmarthenshire rather than city rocking Cardiff. The route is through massed buttercups and dandelion heads as far as the eye can see.

After several fields, a couple of gates and the need to double check which path fork to take (keep the stream beside you) the twin, and by this time massively controversial, reservoirs of Lisvane and Llanishen appear through the trees.

Built in 1886 by the Corporation the reservoirs had a life of unblemished calm and sailing dingy surface until 2004. In that momentous year their then owners, Welsh Water, sold them on to Western Power Distribution – WPD.

Up to then the name WPD meant little to locals. The company managed the power lines. Consumers had no direct contact. WPD's costs were lost in domestic electricity supply invoices from EDF, Scottish Power, EON and the rest. Owned by distant Americans WPD chased profits at the expense of people, nobody realised but that's how it turned out. Their plan was to drain the pair of reservoirs and turn the revealed land along with great slices of the surrounding Nant Fawr Corridor woodland into a housing estate. Traffic flow along previous quiet local cul-de-sacs would rise exponentially. Water fowl together with waxcap fungi, stoneworts, grass snakes and glow worms would be banished to outer darkness. Having their HQ in distant Pennsylvania offered WPD complete protection against local protest. So they thought.

Outraged local residents ran a long, divisive, acrimonious and eventually brilliantly successful campaign against the American giants. The matter became political. There were transatlantic visits and protests at the American home of the chairman. Eventually realising that what turned out to be a decade-long planning battle was costing the company more than future returns might justify the reservoirs were sold. WPD's determined decision maker in Allentown finally gave up. Maybe he was sacked. Lost the strength of his limbs. Couldn't take it anymore. Perhaps he retired. Who cares now? The reservoirs were reacquired in 2016 by Welsh Water and are currently being refilled. Things look up.

Through the trees the reservoirs appear, still double fenced as if this were an atomic research facility, the Lisvane glinting, the Llanishen empty and sprawled with resting birds. There are warning notices against breaking in, against attempting to swim here, and against not being kitted with appropriate protective equipment. Hard hats must be worn. Pedestrians are prohibited. Relief pipelines are being laid. There's also a friendly newsletter in a Perspex case suggesting that Welsh Water are scoping the possibility of opening a visitor centre with café and then providing "Water based activities". A projected reopening date isn't shown. But it's music to local ears.

Lisvane Reservoir

The Nant Fawr Trail, for this is the path we are now on, is hard-topped, waymarked and well maintained. It, too, has Friends and a dedicated bunch they are. Through the Rhyd y Pennau Woods, south of the now demolished Reservoir Keeper's Cottage, is Cliff's Path. This was completed by the Friends in 2011 in memory of their chairman, Cliff Mullins, who died the previous year. It's a rambling trail, appropriate to its dedicatee in the extreme. We snake its flow. If the memorial were a bench then it would rot and dissolve. As it's a path it will remain as long as there are people walking it.

We emerge to cross snarling Rhyd y Pennau Road, just south of the now vanished farm that in the long past was all that stood here. A stroll through Woods Covert, or beside the trees if you prefer sun, pitches us into the open again in front of the De Stijl-like, chequer-cladded Cardiff High and the oval park that holds St Denis' Well, "efficacious in scorbutic complaints", a reed-choked pool below trees. This was once a watering stop on a drovers road. I've taken these waters, splashed my face and supped a small sip. Didn't make any difference that I could discern. The Council have now put up an interpretation board from which all red text has been bleached by the sun.

Over the road, unceremoniously and unmarked, is the meeting place of the Nant Fawr, which we've been sort of following, with Llanishen Brook. Under the Nant Fawr brand the two power on south towards Roath Park Lake and then the new flood defences of Waterloo. But we're at walk end, almost. This walk anyway. A climb up Lake Road North gets us to the Heath Halts with trains to Queen Street from both. Low Level on the former Cardiff Railway also offers trips to Coryton while High Level on the one-time Rhymney railway runs trains back to Lisvane & Thornhill. Edwardian-era industrial rivalry prevented the two lines sharing a stop. As it is the platforms are no further apart than the Bakerloo is from the District at Paddington.

But as this is a Sunday morning scheduled trains have big gaps between them. Gaps a morning long. We retreat instead to the nearby Three Arches, fulsome Sunday lunch beckons. Pub food, "perfection" says Trip Advisor. About right too.

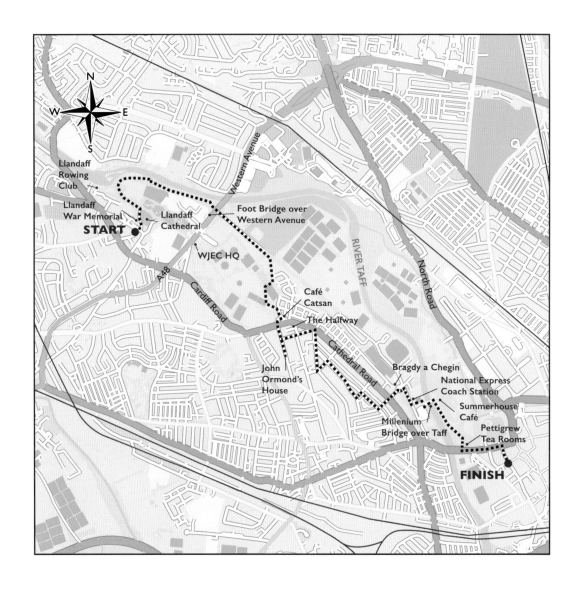

9. THE GREAT STONE

Llandaf Cathedral Green to High Street, Central Cardiff. A walk through the leafy cathedral city taking in the river and its weir. A track across the fields of Pontcanna following the great avenue of limes to criss-cross boho Pontcanna itself with its cafés, eateries and bars. On, then, across Plasturton Gardens to reach what remains Sophia's herbaceous plantings to take the Millennium Bridge over the river. Here we face the flowers of Bute Park before finishing up in High Street where what we have come to see is no longer. The Great Stone a ghost in the air.

Start: Cathedral Green, Llandaf
Finish: High Street/St Mary Street, City centre
Distance 3.4 miles
A slow downhill walk. 25, 63, 63A buses to Llandaff from Westgate Street

www.plotaroute.com/route/628030

There is an air of ancient shimmer at both the start and the end of this walk. Some places in the city turn out to be more susceptible to this than others, regions where history stacks up in great termite piles before toppling back, distraught, into the present. Or is that just my fantasy and it's only like this because the sun is shining. If the day were Cardiff drizzle then the past would get short shrift in the push to get the yomping done. Bit of both I guess.

The Cathedral Green at Llandaf is where we begin, fresh off the bus. It has a preaching cross, a car park, and then a statue of Archdeacon James Rice Buckley in a frock coat and ecclesiastical hat. Beyond him is grass and would be the past personified if it were not for the present leaving the place stuffed with builder's vans, Toyotas and Fords. In the distance stood the Cathedral School which Roald Dahl attended as a boy. On the far side of Goscombe John's War Memorial (two soldiers and a female Celtic chieftain standing on plinths) are the Dean's Steps. We descend their medieval curve towards the river and Ffordd y Meirw (The Way Of The Dead), a path that's not seen a cadaver on the way to burial in a few hundred years since the last one was borne here shoulder high from not too distant Whitchurch.

Ffordd y Meirw is beloved of ghost tour operators who hide behind trees frightening punters with wails and moans. It takes us to the weir, water backed up for the Rowing Club just to the north but originally feeding the mill leat down through the Cathedral Graveyard. Over the river is the site of Gabalfa House, its empty fields now filled with the bricks of a sixties housing estate. As we track south atop the dyke which protects lower land from Taff flood I try out ChirpOMatic[17] which when pointed at the bushes tells me, after a thirty second consideration, that they are full of blackbirds. It offers a picture so I can be sure.

Western Avenue, the A48(M) in its inner city manifestation, is the next barrier. A dual carriage way of non-stop rush barely relieved by traffic light pause further upstream. But there's a footbridge opposite Cardiff Met that gets us across safely and within sight of Jonathan Adams' WJEC HQ which from the bridge looks like a gleaming Ninja Castle.

The long straight-as-a-die path through Pontcanna Fields that we now follow is the hard topped line of the Marquis of Bute's 1880s avenue of limes. It was to run from Sophia Gardens to the south of Llandaff Cathedral where it would terminate in a flourish of oaks and elms in the shape of a 60 foot union jack but the building of Western Avenue put paid that.

This grand avenue takes us past the allotments (where Luke offers new allotment boxes at the bargain price of £6 a time 'laid flat, easily stacked') and the riding stables. A great circle of girls canter in unison as we pass. Open ground to our left heads us south across what are now Llandaff Fields.

This whole green lung of Cardiff appears to have spent its city existence under threat. Over time plans have been laid to build housing estates here, a race track, permanent hard standing for visiting circuses, a zoo, a caravan park, a refugee village, and a fairground. For now it remains green, but keep checking.

Near the much extended and largely open-air Café Castan at the place where the trolley buses used to circle we cross traffic bristling Penhill and roll past the site of the fabled White Shop into Conway Road. For decades in the 60s and 70s this was Cardiff's bohemia central. Poets gathered, film makers debated, and novelists held court at the Conway. The pub has been reborn as the New Conway, still selling beer but also doing a line as part of the Knife and Fork chain of gastro pubs (others include The Discovery, The Pilot and The Old Swan).

Down the road a piece is No 15, a white painted terrace with roses in the front garden and a wall bearing a plaque celebrating the life of John Ormond, poet, 1923-1990. Ormond was a tv film maker for the BBC producing classic films on Ceri Richards, R.S. Thomas, Graham Sutherland and Kyffin Williams. His prize possession was a slightly blurred black and white snap of Dylan Thomas and himself on a beach, proof of cultural ancestry. Ormond's own verse was world class.

After a zip along Mortimer Road and Pontcanna Street we come within range of the legendary Half Way. This traditional Brains house is directly opposite the site of Pontcanna Cottage and the most probable location of the pont (the bridge) over the totally vanished River Canna. The bridge a stone slab and the river little more than a wet ditch. Rumour follows this lost waterway. An acquaintance digging in her basement near here came up with rounded pebbles of the kind found in streams. There was damp on the walls but of the river itself no sign at all.

Plasturton Gardens, Pontcanna

We follow Plasturton Gardens, a suburban boulevard, green centre, grand late Victorian terraces, crossing Plasturton's tiny park to eventually reach Cathedral Road. On the far side, a hundred metres up Sophia Close, one of Bute's Sophia Gardens Lodges hangs on. This is now Bragdy a Chegin (Brewhouse and Kitchen), food and masterclasses in beer. Earlier it was Y Mochyn Du, cwrw, cymraeg, and it's good to see the language roaring on. We cross what was originally the Gardens' ornamental lake to skirt the new

National Express coach station and go over the Taff on the Millennium Bridge.

East–West river crossings are lifeblood to the present city, now that we tire of the time it takes to use a ferry and would never in a million years consider fording at low tide. Not that this river is tidal today anyway. The Cardiff Bay Barrage ended that. At the Millennium Bridge's far side is Summerhouse Café, a worthy place for respite but full today with dog walkers here for the RSPCA Walkies: take your dog for a 4K stroll celebration. In the distance I can hear the amplified voice of the RSPCA mc and behind him a dog-friendly musical thrum.

The path follows Bute Park's rich and enviable herbaceous border. At its southern end is a wooden pole standing like a lone Corinthian column with carved words encircling it. I got 'cynhadledd', 'our', 'cannot' and 'lungs'. There's no nearby interpretative plaque. Tracked on the web I find it to be one of ten Tree Charter Poles sourced from Windsor Great Park and planted across the UK. Ours is in recognition of Cardiff's status as UK tree capital. Tell that to the folk defending wholesale tree removal around Waterloo Gardens.

We exit passing The Pettigrew Tea Rooms, built into another of Bute's lodges, to join the streaming hundreds heading citywards. Our destination is near. That hazy place where High Street meets St Mary Street. It's clear on the maps and, indeed, on the road signs, but a mystery to most Cardiffians. We are now in deep tourist territory where shops facing the Castle sell models of sheep, love spoons made in Korea and have the full version of LlanfairPG pedantically spelled across their window tops.

On the early maps High Street runs between the Castle and the Town Hall. St Mary Street runs from the Town Hall to St Mary's Church, the river bank place of worship washed away by successive Taff floods. When the Town Hall, the first two medieval guildhalls and their third Georgian replacement were in use they were right at Cardiff's centre. Court houses on stilts with the shambles, the meat market, underneath. There was a gaol attached. There were town stocks and a town pump. A town cross. A corn market. A cattle market. A place to meet and a place to carouse. But the whole assemblage was inconveniently right in the centre of the road.

For years the Great Stone of Cardiff was here too. Upon it troths were pledged, oaths sworn, contracts exchanged,

and deals agreed. The historian William Rees[18] says that the Stone "seems to have been in the nature of a public witness." During a time of riot in 1587 the Bailiff called for peace from it and it was used as a marker in matters of land lease and legal claim. It was there when the third town hall was built in 1747 but at some time after that the Great Stone of Cardiff seems to have disappeared.

In the place where it was, or might have been, the centre of pedestrianised High Street, Paddy Power glowering and one those great successes of the present age, a tattoo parlour, standing as witness there's a sense of something. Or is there? When the Stone of Scone vanished from Westminster Abbey in 1950 there was outrage but at the time of the Great Stone's disappearance in rural market town Cardiff no such concern was felt. Where did it go? Too big to be carted it must have been smashed, taken away in broken pieces, used as flood defences, for walls, as foundation for the Victorian fourth town hall where Hodge Building now is. We walk back from that place in space time where it all once shimmered, to get a coffee and Nata cinnamon custard tart in the Portuguese café on Castle Street. Best price in the city.

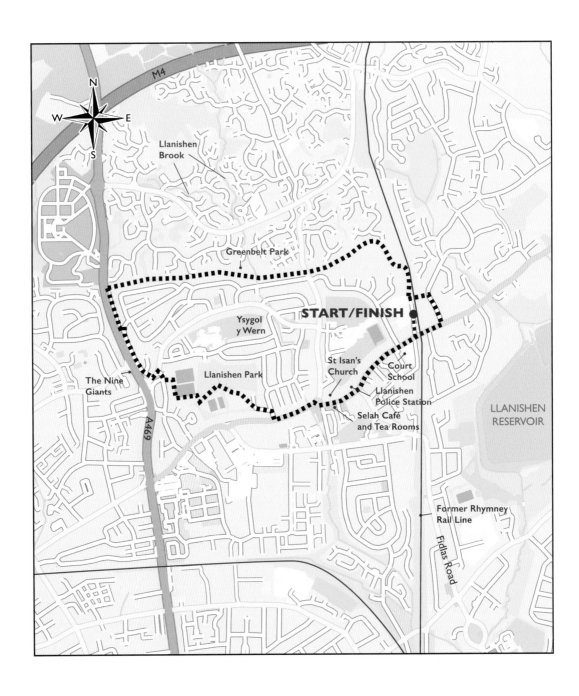

10. GREENBELT

A circular walk around northern Llanishen exploring Greenbelt Park, the fault line between Llanishen and Thornhill, and then returning via Llangranog Shops, Coedcochwyn Wood and Llanishen Park to the centre of Llanishen: St Isan's Church, The Church Inn, welcome cafés and a chip shop and then the rail station from where we set out.

Start and Finish: Llanishen Rail Station
Distance: 3.09 miles
Level. Regular trains to Cardiff Queen Street
(and if you fancy it, Penarth)

www.plotaroute.com/route/605410

Greenbelts might have ancient antecedents but in planning terms they are an invention of the industrial age. Bands of nature around cities as a check against unrestricted sprawl were proposed for London in the 1930s and the idea took hold. For decades Cardiff's best were the ones that separated the city from Newport to the east and Caerphilly to the north. You didn't build in those inviolable strips. Belts were sacrosanct. Untouchable. Until, that is, the need for new housing became so great that they were replaced with more fuzzy designations – green wedges, slabs, slices, rectangles, ovoids and strips. Build where you like just keep plenty of green in the mix. And now, of course, it seems our needs are so great that you don't even have to do that.

John Briggs and I are up near that border at Llanishen rail station. Nearby is a linear park known hardly at all to Cardiffians who do not live nearby. It's a great mile and a quarter fault line that separates 1950s Llanishen from 1980s Thornhill. The two districts might be the same for electoral purposes but as communities they are certainly not.

The greenbelt appears as a vague smudge on most maps, if indeed it appears at all. We reach it from the station by walking up Mill Road and then crossing the former Rhymney Rail line by a stone bridge. Signs warn against horse riding (and in fact keep warning against horse riding for most of our walk). It's as if there has been a plague of such activity, horses at gallop scaring pedestrians, horses leaping local hedges. Horses banging their hooves into kids bikes and leaving long lines of steaming compost among the

Llanishen Rail Station

bushes. A dog walker tells us that actually he hasn't seen a horse anywhere near here in 15 years. The signs obviously work.

The eastern section of Green Belt Park has bulges and bush-filled bends to its linear stretchiness. The houses on each side face each other behind continuous fencing and curtained windows. We don't talk. We don't look. We never do. Berlin East and Berlin West. The border without the guards.

Half way along John and I cross Llanishen Brook just where it dives into the pipework conduit which holds it out of sight all the way south as far as Ty Glas Road. The path meanders ever westwards. In the houses and almost within touching distance full lives are lived but you wouldn't know. Eventually we emerge onto Thornhill itself, buses passing, Caerphilly-bound mountain traffic at its thunderous worst. We are just north of the Nine Giants known now, at least as far as the signboarding tells us, as 'YOUR SIZZLING LOCAL' or 'FREE MEAL THIS FATHER'S DAY'. Maybe there's an older Nine Giants inn sign round the corner but there's certainly nothing on the main road.

The Nine Giants viewed across Thornhill Road

The nine giants were the nine trees planted by the pub's original owner. That was back when the great house here was known as The Lawn. The house's long history with multiple owners and ever-changing name culminated in its purchase by Hancock's Brewery in 1961 and conversion into an earlier version of the child-friendly pub it is today.

We are now walking south. We pass 1950s-built former council houses that have all had their singled glazed metal windows replaced. Some have also had their frontages clad in artificial stone, semis mismatched, naturally, as the competition for the nicest looking rolled.

Edgehill Avenue and Johnston Road give way to Templeton Avenue and any sense of formal estate planning and upkeep vanishes into the sand. On Llangranog Road bright bungalows with hanging baskets and flower-bed dotted lawns mix with two storey blocks of maisonettes. The signs begin again. 'NO BALL GAMES' repeating like a mantra. Gnomes appear in front gardens. Ceramic dogs. Windmills. Characters from Disney. Wagon wheels are fixed to walls. 'Gnome Sweet Gnome' it says on a gate. 'My house was clean last week – sorry you missed it' on another. In a single garden I got as far as 94 in my counting of the kitsch additions before giving up. Bethel Chapel is boarded, its doors and windows showing signs of distress. But as a community centre offering the full range of church-led activities it still operates. More strength to you Rev Pat Clamp even if you too have banned ball games from your premises.

Across the road next to Ysgol Y Wern, the local Welsh-medium primary school, stand a row of terraced shops. Flats above. Balconies. Walls scarred by unpainted repair and broken downpipe. Here embattled Premier Stores still trades. Next door is Lucy Lee's fashion but Lucy has long left this place. Painted figures in 1930s style remain on her shop front. Julie Morgan's constituency office still shows signs of Labour life. Cash4Clothes has a large poster depicting a woman cheeringly holding out a fan of tenners that would have taken two pantechnicons of used shirts to earn.

We turn into Llanishen Park and walk south beside Coed Cochwyn woods staring out across the soccer pitches. The kids' play area is extensive with zip wires and climbing walls. Unvandalised or maybe just well maintained. The path reaches Ty Glas Road and then rolls us into what was once

all there was of Llanishen. St Isan's Norman church. The Church Inn, with its rumoured secret tunnel. An enviable density of stores, cafes and chip shops. And further front gardens complete with gnomes and welcome signs.

We pause at the Selah Café and Tea Rooms which is jam-packed with revellers. A table of workmen are noisily eating full English breakfasts while yelling into their phones. Gaggles of chattering ladies drink lattes with the sofa occupied by whooping babblers who, in another life, would

have been filling the air with Benson breath. We are cheerily served tea in a china tea pot, knitted cosy, bone china cup. Beside me on a shelf is a bone china cake stand laden with knitted cakes. The place is a wonder.

We walk past the Police Station and the ubiquitous local Hyb. The hill rises slowly towards the station from which we started. The houses here are grand. Stone gothic Hill House with red brick The Hollies next door. They were both built in the 1870s. What is now Court School but was once the home of Bishop Headley has chequerboard bands along its upper walls.

At the rail station we get the zooming TfW Sprinter back to Queen Street. Only one stop at Heath Halt but there will be new stations soon. The Metro, ah the Metro. Transport for Wales the future is up to you.

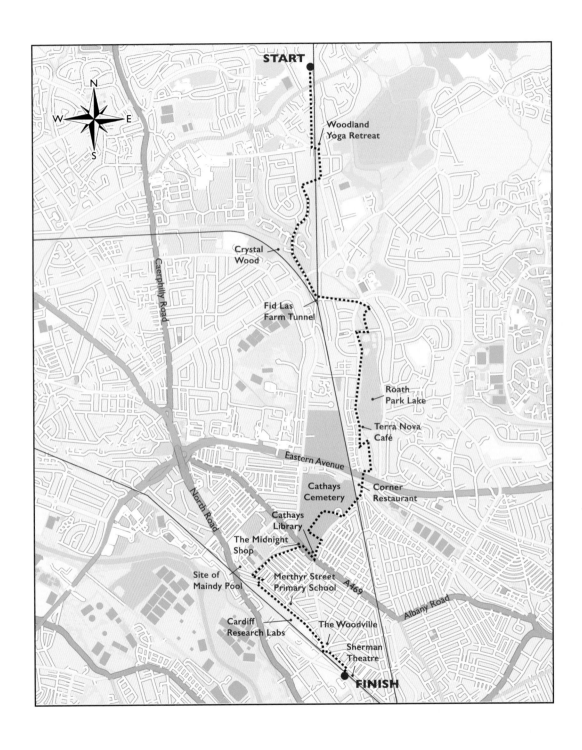

11. LLANISHEN TO CATHAYS

South from an outlying suburb to an inner one. The route takes in Cardiff's celebrated Roath Park Lake and Pleasure Gardens, the now departed Cardiff great and good at Cathays Cemetery and a cycling stadium constructed on an abandoned clay pit before finishing in the city's booming University land.

Start: Llanishen Rail Station
Finish: Cathays Rail Station
Distance: 4.63 miles
Slightly downhill

www.plotaroute.com/route/642315

We walk south from the station down a path that was not created by the heritage industry. Overgrown verge, knee high grass, double set of two-and-a-half metre triple pointed grey steel security railings barely an arms breadth apart. The route follows the railway, arrow straight on its embankment running down to the city. This dyke along which diesels seemingly effortlessly roll was constructed in 1870 from materials excavated from the Caerphilly Rail tunnel. Five vent shafts bored through the hillside. 1600 gallons of water per minute spring discovered in the middle. Numerous deaths. A mile and half long. Took seven years to dig.

John, who'd spent the previous night Morris dancing, is telling me that he's too old for this. "You need a gap in between two activities," he complains. I always thought Morris dancing was gentle and over quickly but maybe not. Then the truth emerges. "I don't think it's actually the dancing. It's more the beer that we use for lubrication." Should have worked that one out. We round past a pocket of brownfield being constructed upon as most corners and niches are in the city now. A guy with a full ZZ Top beard gives us the thumbs up from his dumper truck.

Ahead are the twin arches that carry the railway across Fidlas Road, the pair built at different dates and of differing materials. We go through to pass a high wooden fence fronting the gap between Yapps ever-expanding garage and the embankment. A sign tells us that this is the Woodland Yoga Retreat, singing on Wednesday, yoga the rest of the week. The venue is the 300-year old Bridge Cottage, two

foot thick walls and a CADW listing, but the only way of seeing it is to either take up the Hindu art or send over a drone.

Fidlas Road is bumper to bumper with commuter traffic at nine in the morning. We cross opposite Ewenny Road where the original Fid Las farm house stood to take an arched tunnel under the railway to access Llanishen South Estate. In the days when all this was Bute-owned Bridge Farm land the arch allowed cattle to cross under the tracks. There were gates on both sides each bearing the Bute coat of arms.

Llanishen's South Estate was constructed in the fifties, now much privatised through Thatcher's right to buy but with pockets of overgrown privet and wrecked front gardens plus one house where the owner appears to have chalked her name on the wall by the door.

The way south passes the end of Wingate Drive where for decades poet and architect Ifor Thomas had his Cardiff stronghold. This was a self-built five-bedded detached house with wide corridors and architect-beloved yellow internal doors leading to a first-floor drawing office, a refuge for performance poets before Thomas hung up his performance shoes and escaped west to Solfach. This was all Crystal Wood when the trees still stood. Reaching Lake Road North we pass Heath Halt with its Nextbike rack outside. Full today. No Heath Halt takers.

The road takes us down to the nineteenth century Bute equivalent of Cardiff Bay. A stretch of public water where you least expect one. Roath Park Pleasure Gardens, 130 acres, 30 of them water, has great houses lining its sides. They were built by the Marquis and his fellows in 1887 in order to recoup the cost of the former "malarial bog" they'd donated to the town. The property development game has a long history.

The route crosses the cause of all the trouble, the serpent meandering Nant Fawr stream, to enter the darkness of the Wild Park. This land of the lost at the Lake's top was planned

Roath Park Pleasure Gardens

to house a lake itself although that never happened. There were a number of early twentieth century fish ponds dug at the northern end, long since drained, and there was a hut at the centre, now vanished into the soil. Without good compass skills it's possible in this surprisingly dank and silent place enter the heart of darkness and never escape.

To the south is the Lake itself. The famed islands, five originally but one now missing, sunk or subsumed with the one, as legend has it, on which Jimi Hendrix awoke, stoned, after his first Cardiff gig with the Walker Brothers and Cat Stevens at the Capitol in 1967.

The path tracks lake's edge where geese peck the grass. On the surface algae blooms. It's a hot summer. The café overhanging the water at the south end, Terra Nova, is nothing like the genteel tea shop it could have been. Instead it sells giant slabs of fruit cake, white door-stop rounds of butter-dripping toast and mugs of mighty tea. Their consumption today is accompanied by thundering heavy metal rock. An unexpected mid-morning pleasure. There's a notice on the menu board that reads 'If you are uncertain please speak to a member of staff' but we know just what we want.

Terra Nova Café, Roath Pleasure Gardens

The Prom at Roath Pleasure Gardens

South of the rose garden we exit onto the roundabout where trams once turned, to pass the Corner Restaurant, with its street board advertising 'Beer As Cold As Your Ex's Heart'. Up the harder-than-it-looks slope of Fairoak Road are the 110 acres of Cathays Cemetery. Opened in 1859 this land of the dead was once as much on Cardiff's perimeter as Thornhill Cemetery is now. Entrance is through Thomas and Waring's triple arch pointed gateway, elaborately Gothic, to face the twin and recently restored Victorian Chapels and accompanying bell tower. After decades of decline and abandonment funerals, weddings and community events are again held here. The cemetery they front is a labyrinth of bending paths, sight line blocking trees and counter intuitive junctions.

You can spend a good day here hunting out the last resting places of the great and the Cardiff good. In fact I have. They lie beneath their elaborate monuments lining the principal paths. Such prominence has been paid for. The regular citizenry, whose budgets couldn't run so far, are confined to the grass-filled outlands. William Reardon Smith is here, as are Peerless Jim Driscoll, Bishop Headley, Ernest Willows, John Batchelor, Frances Betty Shand, John Cory, Barry Island Showman John White, Balloon Girl Louisa Maude Evans, ship owner William Tatum and the man who made the parks, Andrew Pettigrew. The Cemetery Friends publish a guide map and several books. But time is pressing, as well as the heat.

Dragon guarding Cathays Library

We exit at the western end next to the recently restored Cathays Library. Endowed by Andrew Carnegie and built in 1906 in an Arts and Crafts style this unexpectedly elaborate structure spreads its two single-storey arms towards the blunder of traffic coming up Crwys Road. Restoration in 2010 has given the City an asset. The library currently houses the City's local history collection formerly available in what is now known as the Central Library Hub on the Hayes.

Our route passes the 1934 Bath stone toilets with their 'MEN' and 'WOMEN' carved divisions supplemented by a metal sign declaring 'Ladies' just in case you were unsure. Not that any of this matters. The facility is chained and if the money were found to reopen it may well have to be gender neutral. The future is not the past.

Over the road is the Midnight Shop. Here we buy water from smiling and bindi-wearing Indians, Mr and Mrs Upadhyat, whose joyful sales-pitch and ready posing for photographs sets us up for the hot stroll along Gelligaer Street to the edge of Maindy Stadium.

Management of the stadium now complete with velodrome track and indoor swimming has, like all City leisure provision, been farmed out to the private sector. The company are known hopefully as Better. The stadium was built in the 1920s on the site of Maindy Pool, the water-filled remains of earlier clay pits. It was first a park plus tennis courts, getting its cinder running tracks and 460 metre cycle track later. Just as well the velodrome component did arrive. This is where, as a member of the Maindy Flyers, Tour de France 2018 winner Geraint Thomas trained.

The route turns south now where the brickworks stood to run along Maindy Road passing what was Cathays Yard and the carriage works of the Taff Vale Railway. St Monica's School with its church tower directly ahead is now Merthyr Street Cardiff Muslim Primary School marking the district's continuing subtle demographic shift.

Turn the corner, though, and one of the City's more recent dramatic changes pushes into view. Here stand the extensive and architecturally sparkling new research labs of Cardiff University. They are great in number and unanticipated in extent. The Brain Research Imaging Centre, the Cognitive Neuroscience Laboratories, the European Cancer Stem Cell Research Institute, the MRC Centre for Neuropsychiatric Genetics and Genomics and the Department of Optometry and Vision Sciences. Their structure, leafy landscaping, and coloured solar cladding, offer a quiet thrill. Lidl is still there at the Woodville Road end as is the ever reliable Woodville pub, 'Wednesday wings for 25p each', 'Craft beers £3 every Thursday'. On the wall outside someone mixing English and Welsh with a certain fluid invention has chalked the words 'QUEER PŴER'.

We cross onto Senghenydd Road with the Sherman Theatre at its half way point to access the train again at Cathays Station. This time the line is the former Taff Vale Railway that connects Cardiff with Merthyr. Is it worth catching the diesel pacer one stop to Queen Street? Certainly not. I cross the footbridge and head south along Park Place. Five minutes. Walk's end, city centre.

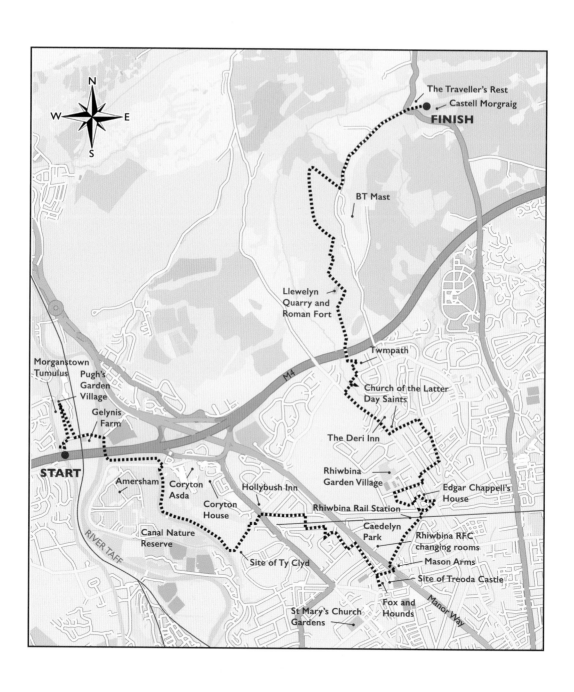

The Traveller's Rest
Castell Morgraig
FINISH

BT Mast

Llewelyn Quarry and Roman Fort

Twmpath

Church of the Latter Day Saints

The Deri Inn

Rhiwbina Garden Village

Edgar Chappell's House

Rhiwbina Rail Station

Caedelyn Park

Rhiwbina RFC changing rooms

Mason Arms

Site of Treoda Castle

Fox and Hounds

Manor Way

St Mary's Church Gardens

Morganstown Tumulus

Pugh's Garden Village

Gelynis Farm

START

Amersham

Coryton Asda

Coryton House

Hollybush Inn

Canal Nature Reserve

Site of Ty Clyd

RIVER TAFF

M4

N
W   E
S

12. MORGANSTOWN TUMULUS TO CASTELL MORGRAIG

If an urban hike takes a while and has lots of diversions then this is certainly a good example. A walk along the defensive line between four of Cardiff's lesser-known forts and castles. Expect mounds and evocative spaces, canals and lost railways, suburban streetscapes and industrial relics, easy pavement strolls and muddy struggles through woods. Morganstown to the top of Caerphilly Mountain via Whitchurch and Rhiwbina with plenty of drop out spots for those who prefer the shorter trail.

Start: Pugh's Garden Centre, Morganstown
Finish: Castell Morgraig (The Traveller's Rest)
Distance: 7.09 miles
The early section is mostly level but with some muddy inclines in the Glamorgan Canal Local Nature Reserve. Pugh's is about a mile away from both Radyr and Taffs Well rail stations. 63 bus stops almost outside. The section from Rhiwbina Station north involves a full hill climb but this is not too strenuous. Return is on the 25 bus to Cardiff centre

www.plotaroute.com/route/588368

I'm at Pugh's Garden Centre (or Garden Village as they now style it), below the Lesser Garth. This is the far end of Morganstown. I haven't come here for plants but I do try out a swift Americano in their café before I set out on this castle-seeking hike. Fortifications from the period of the Norman invasion a thousand years ago still litter our landscape. A few are native Welsh but most belong to the conqueror. Stone castles, stone keeps, moats and great earthen ramparts. The big local examples which we all know – Cardiff, Castell Coch, Caerphilly – run in a defensive arc. The Normans squatted on the rich lands of the coast. The native Welsh ran a never-ending guerrilla campaign from the hills to the north.

Filling in the arc were a series of defensive towers and palisaded mounds. These were the Norman equivalent of the armoured watch towers that crossed sectarian Belfast. These mottes, as the mounds were called, were usually surrounded by water-filled moats and defensive ditches. The protected space was the bailey. What has survived through the centuries is not much with most levelled and their land built on but at least two still remain intact.

The first is at the end of Morgantown's football field, half-hidden in trees and massively overgrown with bramble. It may be 18 feet high and 120 feet round but against the background of the rising densely-shrubbed Garth it's pretty difficult to see. There's no celebratory sign nor easy way to climb to the top. Morganstown tumulus, accessible by the intrepid and viewable only if you know just where it is.

Access is through the alley at the side of Pugh's or down the lane from Ty Nant Road. A lone dog walker engrossed in her phone crosses the bogland of the rugby pitch when I visit. The skateboard park alongside the main rail line back to the city is deserted.

Gelynis Farm

I track riverwards traversing the rail link on an unmanned crossing to pass Gelynis Farm[19] and its vineyard. This ancient house was built in 1570 by Pentyrch iron master Hugh Lambert although what you see today is mostly repair and later addition, the accretions of four and half centuries of wear and weather. For years Gelynis was managed as a pick-your-own venture, squally kids and lumbering adults getting their fingers juicy on strawberries and raspberries and then having tea and pop in the café. Today it's a b&b.

Beyond it is an iron bridge across the Taff that also carries a water main. It's wide enough for a mounted cyclist to traverse without dismounting, just. On the far side is the Taff Trail. I turn right, south, to use a few hundred metres of this well signposted long distance bridleway to get myself below the elevated M4. The concrete bridge sides are graffitied with the usual thrown up sprawl of angular tags and swirling colours this time with the addition of a speech bubble saying 'This Is Fine', and so it is.

I turn east at the first opportunity to follow Longwood Drive through the trees. I'm on a path sandwiched between the ever-flowing M4 and the Amersham medical isotope facility at Forest Farm. After a few hundred metres and just west of Coryton Asda (although the shopping giant remains invisible through the trees) I cross the Drive to enter the sign boarded Glamorganshire Canal Local Nature Reserve.

Anti-development campaigners have been in action here. There's a plastic-sleeved notice fixed to a fence post that protests Velindre Hospital's proposed expansion onto land just to our south which will involve the loss of Whitchurch Meadow forever. Cancer treatment vs the future of the planet. It's a tough call.

I avoid the canal, the last surviving water-filled section of what was once an essential industrial artery carrying coal and iron ingots from the producing valleys to the exporting Cardiff docks. Instead I climb rising ground to the cutting that once held the Cardiff Railway. This was a Bute venture set up in 1898 in direct competition to the Taff Vale Railway in the fight for coal exporting dominance. Bute who already owned Cardiff Docks also wanted to own the method of dock supply. But his new railway failed. Its remains, single tracked, currently terminating at Coryton. Metro developers are already talking about putting it back so that the line will run on to Pontypridd.

The Middle Path, paralleling the cutting, and along which I am bound is hardly a Buddhist thing. In place of ease and balance I get mud and slide, tree grapple and bush snag. But the views of the pools, feeders and water-filled canal through the still leafless trees (it's March) are splendid.

Eventually I hit a path junction right where Ty Clŷd farmhouse stood and where the Melin Griffith feeder joined the Glamorgan Canal. Here I turn left, north, into Coryton. Coryton is Whitchurch actually, but Cardiffians like to be creative about saying just where it is they live. Coryton House, after which the district was named, was the grand home of Herbert, son of John Cory, the Victorian-era Cardiff shipping magnate. His ornamental gardens still exist although the house has been converted into a school.

To my left as I slither on are the apartment towers that offer social housing to this part of the north city. The path reaches the main Merthyr Road beside what might be a park (or might not). In the not yet sprung spring it's hard to tell. There are couple of benches, only lightly vandalised, a green bin-bagged bin, and a green triangle of grass surrounded by rough encroaching undergrowth. On the far side of the main road is the Hollybush Inn, now operated by Stonehouse as a Pizza and Carvery (Hand Carved Roasts, Help Yourself Veg and Roasties). Carveries do well out here in the far Cardiff fringe.

By now the suburban atmospherics have changed. Gone is any sense of nature, river corridor, water meadow, field or grass lung. The replacement is calm conurbation, silence surrounded by the distant hum of traffic from Cardiff's périphérique. I'm on Lon y Celyn, paralleling the Coryton railtrack. Someone has a red phone box in their front garden, others have pots and bird baths, benches and gnomes.

At what was originally a run of shops, now mostly empty apart from La Beauty Boutique Hairdressers on the corner,

I turn south into a lane which crosses the railway to drop me on Park Avenue. "What district am I in?" I ask a woman with a shopping bag. "Whitchurch". This reply is given with a definitiveness which suggests that I should know this and not need to ask. I wind on, along St John's Crescent and then St Margaret's Road, to trickle out onto Heol y Forlan near its junction with Old Church Road.

This is innermost ancient Whitchurch. The old church being St Mary's, the white church, demolished in 1904, its sixteenth century graveyard turned into an unexpected garden where gravestones flourish among the greenery, weathered old, serifed and silent. In the car park between the new(ish) Catholic Church of St Teilo's and the now extended Fox and Hounds was once a great castle. In the form of an earthen tumulus, Tre-Oda is clearly shown on Victorian maps. On twentieth century ones it's gone. Whatever might have been left of the mound and its archaeological remains were finally disposed of when Treoda flats were constructed in the 1960s and the pub car park extended back with a layer of unforgiving tarmac. But the castle is still there, in my head, its wooden keep ever watching out for the encroaching enemy.

As lost castles go this one has certainly been wiped from the face of the earth. There's no memorial, no sign, no nameplate, no recalling of its existence in local house name nor street sign. The pub could offer a castle burger but they don't.

I cross Manor Way, Northern Avenue, called here for unaccountable reasons Ash Grove, to enter Caedelyn Park along the side of an electricity substation and the fast flowing Rhydwaedlyd Brook. I've avoided the Mason's Arms, now a huge Toby Carvery, where the entrance signboarding has their entire offer – Travelodge, Toby Carvery, Home of the Roast, in larger type than the pub's actual name. Today their special is a Freakshake which, when I look it up, turns out to contain enough calories to power a football team.

In the park the extensive green is given over almost exclusively to sport. 'Rhiwbina RFC' it says across the top of a white blockhouse. At the park's eastern end is the footbridge to Rhiwbina Station. 'Adopted by Rhiwbina Amateur Theatrical Society' reads a sign. The footweary could diesel it back to Queen Street from here. Trains are frequent and you get to see a different city from their windows. The still enthusiastic have rising hills before them. I step on.

Rhiwbina. The name sounds ancient and in ways it is. Through the years it has been many things, from Rubinay to Rubina, from Riw Beine to Rhiewbyna, and Riw'r Beyne to Rhywbanau. Edgar Chappell, the Cardiff historian, whom I'd been reading before setting out on this trip, has a theory that the name derives not from the Welsh for 'the hill slope of Ina' or some suchlike, but from Riu Brein, the name for a Rhiwbina Hill farmstead as recorded in the eleventh century *Book of Llandav*. On who or what *Riu Brein* might have been Chappell doesn't speculate. He gets round much of the naming problem by incorporating Rhiwbina into the district I've just walked through for his excellent history of the area, *Old Whitchurch*. Not that this white-housed Hampstead of Cardiff is anything other than Rhiwbina now.

From the station the route is briefly east to the Beulah Road junction where the Rhydwaedlyd brook is culverted under the traffic lights before turning into Lon Fach to access the Garden Village. The lane passes a 1920s style slate-roofed Hobbit-hut called The Wendy House, originally the Garden Village Residents Association meeting room and still in use for community activities.

Rhubina Fields, a Garden Village, was Cardiff's Port Sunlight, a socialist vision from the 1910s where decent living conditions for poorer people would be provided at a reasonable price. Houses would be modest. There would be open spaces, private gardens, hedges and trees, indoor bathrooms, damp proof courses. The enterprise would run on a co-operative basis. No one would own their homes but all would have shares in the company. The movement was fronted by Prof H. Stanley Jervons. Edgar Chappell, on the council now, was a committee member.

The original plan was for a thousand houses, "From Work to Home by Train or Bus. Gardening – Tennis – Country Walks". The centrepiece was Y Groes, white fronted Tyrolean-rendered houses surrounding a village green. The atmosphere, even today, is quite unlike anything anywhere else in the city. Unhurried calm. Decluttered, clean and bright.

On one of these slate-roofed semis is a blue plaque – 'Edgar Leyshon Chappell, Author, Alderman and early Rhiwbina Garden Village Resident lived here 1914-1924'. He's following me round. The Garden Village with its grass and endless whiteness got up to more than 300 houses before wars and societal change saw its principle off. The Company was wound up in 1968.

There are plaques everywhere. The teetotal founder of St Fagans, Iorwerth Peate, lived here as did the great Welsh novelist Kate Roberts. "Fewer homes for the needy poor more home of the middle-class intelligentsia," suggests Chappell. He also comes up with a few other soubriquets: "Little Moscow" and "Bolshiville" (due to the large number of Socialist politicians using co-operative Rhiwbina for

photoshoots), and "Debtors' Retreat" (due to new residents escaping here from outstanding financial obligations elsewhere).

From Y Groes I cross Lon y Dail to take the lane on to Parc y Pentre. On the far side of this communal green is Lon Isa which points east to eventually get me again to that belting Taff-tributary, the Rhydwaedlyd Brook. An unsurfaced path runs parallel, heading north, past flood monitoring equipment and remote CCTV to reach Heol Llanishen Fach and the great God-pointing edifice of the Church of the Latter-day Saints. These Christian Primitivists, the Mormons, baptise the dead and send their white-shirted emissaries into our towns and cities where, with never ending politeness, they try to convince us of their cause. Their north Cardiff HQ has all the markings of a mega church but today deserted. It's Thursday. God will be back at the weekend.

At the corner with Rhiwbina Hill I walk north. It's a slow rise passing the Deri Inn (Ember Inns Pale Ale) and the Deri Stores. This has turned itself into a suburban garden centre to judge from the serried plants offered for sale outside.

A few hundred yards further a public footbath turns east off Rhiwbina Hill. Take care not to miss it. This one is narrow and has a giant Leylandii hedge on its lefthand side. Leylandii in their giantness have become a suburban obsession. How many have you seen blocking light in an assertion of green credentials and a desire for privacy. The path crosses the Nant Nofydd,

a Rhydwaedlyd tributary, to lose itself in a garden jumble of fences and wooden back doors. Keep looking. One of these, ahead to the right, has both an openable latch and a sign with an arrow on it showing the way ahead. I go through. This is the top of Lon Ysgubor. A path heads north crossing the churned mud of what was once the farmland of Ynys-yr-ysgallen-fraith.

I am now on open ground with the rising slopes of the Wenallt on the far side of the M4. The centrepiece here is Rhiwbina's claim to medieval fame – the Twmpath. This earthen and much overgrown tumulus is clearly a Norman-era motte much in the style of the one at Morganstown but bigger, much. Access up the steep sides is possible although I fall over twice getting my legs caught in encroaching bramble. Myth says that eleventh century local chieftain Iestyn ap Gwrgant is buried here and that there is treasure at the mound's centre. Gold and jewels but cursed. Dig and the devil will smite you. Infect your skin, burn your insides. In 1849 archaeologists led by F. Fox Esq. opened the mound to find 'excessively offensive black peaty matter' at the centre with 'something like a piece of iron' within. Among his papers F. Fox Esq. leaves no record of then being smitten by satanic fire.

Rhiwbina Twmpath

I cross the surrounding green, heading north. A pedestrian bridge with stiles at both ends goes over the M4 to gain the rising hill. A small corrugated metal covered reservoir, a new iron age intruder, is visible through the trees.

Rather than wild country this whole area is actually parkland, acquired by the Council in 1924 and tidied up for Cardiffians although in recent years cuts have seen maintenance reduced to a minimum. Wenallt Hill itself is bountiful in its waymarkings. They are everywhere and point in all directions. Paths for horses and for pedestrians to all destinations. I am looking now for the next stronghold in this quintet of fortifications, this time iron age, or Roman, or maybe both. It's there, above, on the Wenallt Ridge. The paths rise. I take the middle one, Buddhist as ever.

The Llewelyn Quarry (more properly The Gelli Quarry) and its attendant stone crushing equipment was once here too. Slap in the middle of the ancient earthworks. Back when the Llewelyn family started extracting stone in the nineteenth century planning was clearly lax. The quarry went out of business in 1934.

Access is easiest by heading straight up the slope although given the continuing proliferation of paths before me alternatives are certainly possible. What remains of the quarry is a greened over gash in the hillside, like a drift mine. Around it what remain of the embankments of the earlier iron age fort and Roman camp are clearly visible. Roman pottery and coins have been found and the ramparts show signs of stone revetment. Today there are ropes used by kids to swing out over the ditches but with a refreshing lack of cans and half-burned detritus. The offspring of the Rhiwbina Bolshiville residents who frequent this place know respect. Wenallt peace everywhere.

Although it is hard to discern in the darkness of the birch wood this one-time camp and fort actually sits on a promontory. Before the trees took over there would have been sweeping views over the Cardiff floodplain below. But these are managed woodlands now and I weave on through what in season becomes a sea of frothy bluebell blue.

Beyond a picnic stop car park edging the tarmac of Wenallt Hill two huge BT communication masts can be seen through the trees. Telecoms are often shrouded in secrecy and these two are no exception. They are protected by double razor fencing, CCTV and a brash spume of warning signs. At their feet can be glimpsed what remains of the Wenallt war rooms from the 1950s. Half submerged in the hillside these alien cold war relics were set up for use as a command and control bunker in the event of nuclear attack. Visits would be fascinating but they are inaccessible and still largely forbidden territory. The adventurer, Will Millard, was seen enter them on a climbers rope, torch in hand, for an episode of Lazerbeam's *Hidden Cardiff* (BBC TV) last year. What he found was a creaking, broken, and plaster-filled future that, thank god, never happened.

At hill's top the treescape of Coed y Wenallt gives way to farmland and the route on is either by taking a great loop of path downslope and back along the woodland's edge or simply tracking the road. It's been at least seven miles and a few hours since I set out so I take the easier option. Fields have horses and mud. Sheep bleat in the distance. This is absolutely no longer the city.

North of Wenallt Farm the woodland path re-joins Wenallt Road just ahead of the junction at Thornhill with the A469, the main route over Caerphilly Mountain. Caerphilly Borough Council can't wait to claim ownership and has a huge 'Croeso Welcome' sign. The Maesycymmer Bank Holiday Boot Sale advertises itself on the side of a fence surrounding the ancient stone cottage of Hafod Y Milgi.

Over the road is the Traveller's Rest which has sold beer here for centuries. These days it's almost exclusively full plate dinners with triple-cooked chips a speciality. It's what beyond it that has drawn me here. This walk has followed a line of Norman Fortifications: Cardiff, Morganstown, Tre-Oda, The Twmpath and now Castell Morgraig. It lies ruined and moss-covered in the trees just to the east of the tavern. Access is over the fence at the rear of the car park – technically a trespass – and then fifty yards on through the bushes. An alternative route is available along a path a hundred metres downhill on the Cardiff side.

The overgrown Castell Morgraig

There are sections of stone block still visible, worked stone that made the five towers and a section of curtain wall. It's all hugely jumbled and overgrown and considerably less visible as a castle than it was the last time I came here during the winter of 2010. Morgraig is subject to much dispute. Are these the remains of a Welsh castle? Were they ever actually completed? Isn't this the start of another Norman fortification in the long string that runs to Caerphilly, one that was interrupted mid-construction and never finished? Who can be sure?

The ruins stand on the fault line which, in the thirteenth century, separated Welsh Senghenydd from Anglo-Norman Glamorgan. A line in the ground. Was this a de Clare-built fortification or a piece of Welsh defiance put up in support of fourteenth century rebellion? CADW have discovered two now collapsed defensive towers further east along the ridge and are certain Morgraig was Norman. Unofficial Welsh investigators disagree. Among the rampaging bushes and protruding bramble it's almost impossible to tell but you can take a view. I've taken mine. We look north into the hills of Wales, the flat of Cardiff to our backs.

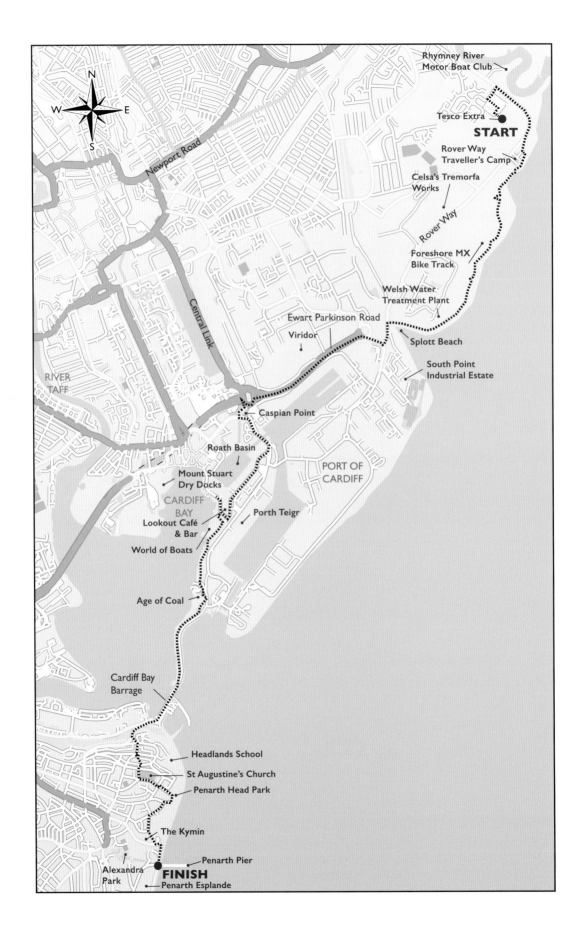

Rhymney River
Motor Boat Club

Tesco Extra
START

Rover Way
Traveller's Camp

Celsa's Tremorfa
Works

Rover Way

Foreshore MX
Bike Track

Welsh Water
Treatment Plant

Ewart Parkinson Road

Viridor

Splott Beach

South Point
Industrial Estate

Caspian Point

Roath Basin

PORT OF
CARDIFF

Mount Stuart
Dry Docks

CARDIFF
BAY

Porth Teigr

Lookout Café
& Bar

World of Boats

Age of Coal

RIVER
TAFF

Newport Road

Central Link

Cardiff Bay
Barrage

Headlands School

St Augustine's Church

Penarth Head Park

The Kymin

Penarth Pier

Alexandra
Park

FINISH

Penarth Esplande

13. TESCO EXTRA PENGAM GREEN TO PENARTH PIER

A mainly coastal walk starting on the banks of the River Rhymney, tracking through the disparate wonders of Cardiff Bay, crossing the Barrage and then climbing over Penarth Head to finish at the tip of Penarth Pier

Start: Car park Tesco Extra Pengam Green (61 bus)
Finish: Penarth Pier (return by train from Penarth Station just up the hill to Cardiff Central)
Distance 5.96 miles
Mainly level but with a steep climb over Penarth Head. This walk can be broken after 3.67 miles at the Lookout Café and Bar in Cardiff Bay (Baycar bendy-bus back to city centre)

www.plotaroute.com/route/528947

The Tesco Extra car park is built on the site of the Rover Works. Before the cars were made here this was Cardiff Aerodrome doubling as RAF Pengam Moors during the war. In the rough land over the bund to the store's west you can still find traces of the runway tarmac. The store manager, ever vigilant, wants to know why I'm taking photos of the low autumn sun streaming through his store sign, lighting it like a pre-Raphaelite jewel. When I tell him that it's for a book and in it I'll be recommending his café's all-day Cumberland sausage breakfast he smiles, placated. We have the breakfast too and for supermarket food it isn't bad at all.

This walk to the estuary coast on the fringes of the built-up city is about as long as they get in *Walking Cardiff*'s selection. I explain this to John as we exit east by the car park lights to gain the Wales Coast Path running down alongside the mud of the Rhymney River. To our west the almost cloudless blue of the sky is supplemented by pillars of white from the slag reclamation plant next to Celsa's Tremorfa Works. The white is mixed with a swirl of black from the burning tyres outside the Rover Way Gypsy Camp. Blazing rubber is almost a permanent feature in these parts, an eco-act of refuse incineration or permissible vandalism, who knows.

At low tide the extensive river mud glistens better than party jelly. You can't imagine crossing it but members of the

Rhymney River Motor Boat Sail and Angling Club

Rhymney River Motor Boat Sail and Angling Club clearly do. Members' boats and floating gangways strew the riparian gleam. Reed covered land flattens out towards the estuarine Severn. The remains of wrecked sofas and broken chipboard poke up between the grass. Two gypsy ponies, inquisitive and on long tethers, push their noses into John's camera. If it were not for the constant thrum and thrash of the mostly out of sight traffic along Rover Way you could imagine yourself lost in some rural idyll. But, no, this is still the city.

Ahead, as the path turns from following the Rhymney to tracking the Severn itself, are the single-storey sloping roofs of the gypsy encampment. The frequency of charcoal burned earth and dumped hard core increase as we near but never enough to actually impede progress. The establishment of the Coast Path running yards away on the seaward side of the camp provoked controversy when it was opened in 2012. There were lurid tales of gypsy proposals to block access and Council plans to install a sixteen-foot-high privacy fence that none of the 21-pitch site's occupants wanted. All that appears to have faded and there's no one about as we pass.

The path climbs on through a forest of buddleia to the seaward side of the Council's large Foreshore MX bike track[20]. Way above Kawasaki rip and roar but on our path you can barely hear a sound. In fact out of the sight of anything urban and certainly anything even vaguely industrial this could be Carmarthen Bay. John looks out to sea and asks if Dylan Thomas' Boathouse will soon hove into view. The world here has that sense. But it doesn't last. The steam rising from Celsa's slag reduction plant again begins to mark the approaching horizon. A passing Irish-accented local, walking with his son, says it's a good day for it. "You'll see them up ahead," he advises. "Yellow trucks. We collect metal, see. It's what we do."

And we do indeed encounter two battered and yellow painted motorised dumpers driven by big men wearing facemasks headed towards the foreshore. They forage for pig iron waste among the lost clinker, gobs and clusters that can be melted and used again.

The brief rurality has now given way to fully-fledged industrial wham. This is the place Des Barry called the zone[21]. A disconnected land, impenetrable, out of time and in a location you least expect it be. Below us great mounds of steaming steel plant slag are probed by giant diggers. Water sprays and steam gushes in great clouds. This is how all the industrial world used to be. I feel like Dic Penderyn arriving at the Ynysfach Iron Works in Cordell's *The Fire People*.

Welsh Water's Waste Water Treatment Plant

Industry continues, albeit in more restrained and well-fenced form, as the path runs behind Welsh Water's Dan Dare-looking Waste Water Treatment and Green Energy Facility. On a bad day you can smell the activity here but not this morning. Since we've begun with the boathouse John and I continue the theme with a discussion of Berryman and his DT memorial poem, published posthumously. In it Dylan invites Berryman to visit him at his 'Edna Millay' cottage at Laugharne. There they can "down a many few". The malt, he meant. Both dead from it by the time the poem appeared.

Rounding what serves for a headland on this strip of coast you can see the Heliport and the line of big box prefabs that form South Point Industrial Estate. If you approach this industrial estate from the city along Foreshore Road you'll encounter sign after sign that warn against access to the actual shore. None available. No passage. Keep out. Cardiffians barred from their own sea line.

Just in front of the estate is the mythical Splott Beach. I brought Brendan Burns here a few years back. His studio wasn't much more than a mile away which made him the beach's nearest artist. I wondered if the painter of the Druidstone shoreline might find some more local inspiration but that doesn't seem to have happened yet.

What serves for beach is actually a sewer outfall washing mud and slurry seawards. There's a patch of what might be sand, grey black and, on a dry day, fine enough to run through your fingers. But it's hardly convincing evidence of a lost Cardiff past when this place might have streamed with paddling day-trippers, deck chair sitters and ice cream sellers, back then before the industrial revolution. In fact if you check old(er) maps you'll find that as recently as the start of the twentieth century this place was still sea. We are on re-claimed land. The sea might rise but round here it also falls.

The coastal path dumps us at the tail end of Rover Way, 40 mph traffic still thundering. The faint of heart could track back here along the noisy and incredibly dirty roadside to where we started and wash themselves down in Tesco toilets before celebrating with a latte. But John and I are tougher and we walk on to the Ocean Way roundabout to reach the pedestrian edge of Cardiff's latest road. This is the A4232 Eastern Bay Link, now renamed Ffordd Ewart Parkinson after the city's famous planning officer. The Parkinson highway rises on its stilts to rush along the top edge of the Roath Dock with the futuristic-looking Viridor Waste Incinerator Plant, its roof mimicking the curve of the WMC, beyond. This dominates the skyline much as the Spiller's flour mill at the end of the Roath Dock once did. You can't see much seawards here because of the road bridge's protecting wall but holding a camera over the top like a periscope and randomly snapping reveals a line of skips surrounding great cone tops of sorted scrap metal.

Roath Basin

The mud and bramble of the coast hitherto has now given way to massed development. Our route drops down past Cardiff Waterside's base at Caspian Point to enter what the marketing world now calls Porth Teigr (a Welsh mangling of Tiger Bay) but was once home to the countless coal staithes of Roath Basin. The land, like the dock itself, is currently empty but will soon house a hotel, further apartments, and Box City, a development of shops, offices and pop-up markets to be built Lego-like from shipping containers. To our immediate south is the baroque front of the BBC's Roath Lock studios where they make everything from *Casualty* to *Dr Who*. My wife, Sue, reports spotting Duffy on Cardiff Central station and I've seen Cybermen in nearby Mount Stuart Square. So keep your eyes open.

We stop at the Lookout Café and Bar, refreshments served with some style from an actual shipping container situated on the edge of the road on to the Barrage. If you want to collapse then wait here a while before catching a bendy-bus from the nearby stop back up to city centre. Otherwise it's forward towards a different country.

The walk on from the home of the coffihead with its double deck chairs and giant homemade pasties is past World of Boats and the blue roof of the now closed Dr Who Experience. We skirt a corner of land reclaimed in 1907 during the building of the Queen Alexandra Dock to reach a much longer stretch reclaimed almost a hundred years later. Here a great sea dam has been built. This is the Cardiff Bay Barrage. The idea for this £200m engineering project came to Freddie Watson, a little known Welsh Office bureaucrat and advisor to Margaret Thatcher's Secretary of State for Wales, Nicholas

Edwards, in 1985. In a moment of vision uncharacteristic of the civil service he suggested blocking off the whole of Cardiff's most muddy and massively tidal bay with a concrete and stone dike. This would have a road on top which would run from the edge of the Queen Alexandra Dock in the east to Penarth Head in the west. Given the £200m cost and not inconsiderable engineering difficulties (managing the outfall of two rivers and the estuary's unbelievably large tidal rise and fall) a seemingly impossible dream. But such things do occasionally come to pass. After much unfounded fear, objection from everywhere in the country that wasn't the capital, as well as a lot from the capital itself, the Barrage impounding the Bay opened in 1999. The names Cardiff Docks and Tiger Bay were relegated to the city's colourful past. That new bland invention, the beachless and unexpectedly fresh water Cardiff Bay was born.

We pass the Bute and then the Mount Stuart Dry Docks which stand empty now that their ship repair trade has collapsed. The Barrage snakes ahead. Plans proposed for transportation along its top have been many. When the Butetown Historical Railway Society was at Bute Road Station there was a pitch to track a steam railway across the Barrage all the way to sunny Penarth. Cardiff Trolley enthusiasts suggested running rescued and refurbished buses from the Maritime Museum to Penarth Marina. Others proposed a driverless metro or a cutting edge vacuum tube monorail. Some even suggested, perish the thought, that we could have a road, a new fast route from city to Vale. In the end we got none of these. Instead they built a cycle path and pedestrian walkway along which a tourist road train looking like Thomas the Tank Engine would run. Not today though, summer has gone.

Seawards, embraced by the slanting sun's rays, are the islands of Flat and Steep Holm – one a part of North Somerset, the other constitutionally Cardiff. Between them a containership of cars fresh from Portbury slowly moves, a third Holm, bathed in lines of light. "Les jambes du soleil" John calls these. *The legs of the sun.*

Half way across are clustered Barrage attractions, things best enjoyed on days when the winds are low. South westerlies can belt over the bay waters here, churning them into fighting shapes. Like the jaws of tigers, as visiting Portuguese mariners were alleged to say. There's the *Age of Coal,* an outdoor exhibition of miniature pit heads, coal trucks and stacks of anthracite slack. Next door is a basketball

court and a climbing wall labelled in perfect English 'impossible is nothing'. Wall paintings of tigers creep along the edge of the Bae Teigr Skateboard Park. A life-size model of Roald's Enormous Crocodile sits beside the path smiling.

More tigers appear at this point in the shape of a snow dog painted to look like one. The Portuguese have something to answer for. Beyond, on the headland's ridge, are what were once the celebrated Billy Banks, a series of council managed high-rises that, from the Cardiff distance, resembled teeth. Singer John Lewis made a rockabilly album inside them, *The Billy Banks Sessions*. Sales have been slow. The district has been regenerated, gentrified, and rebranded up-market as Penarth Heights.

The Barrage lock gates and fish pass, the working centre of its 0.68 mile length, is actually at the Penarth end. Here are sluices, estuary side mud banks, fish ladders, locks and spillways. Felice Varini's truly impressive public artwork of massive yellow circles spanning the tops of the gates and lifters is beginning to look worn and faded. Out at Estuary side the yacht club's pink control hut has also lost much of vibrant colour. As a city we make things new and bright and then, where others might maintain, we simply allow time to wear our creations into fade and disrepair.

The climb along Paget Road up Penarth Headland is steep but that doesn't stop runners and at least one intrepid cyclist in helmet and tights. The road reaches the bulk of Headlands, a hotel built in 1868 for a trade that never somehow materialised. It's been a children's home and special school since the war. At hill's top, skirting St Augustine's Church and the grave of Joseph Parry (composer of 'Myfanwy') the apartments of Mariners Heights look back at the Dinky-toy spread of Cardiff Bay.

At Penarth Head Park, reached along Penarth Head Lane, the scruffy space with the Bristol Channel's greatest views has been significantly upgraded. In place of a crumbling set of benches there is now a circular Penarth Head Viewing Platform with artist Maureen O'Kane's dragon's tail mosaic seat as its centrepiece. From here on a good day you can see everything from Cardiff Docks (1 mile) to Weston-super-Mare (10 miles). There is also a hopeful direction arrow pointing at Penarth's twin town St Pol-de-Leon (193 miles). For the true psychogeographic walker you can also face the other way and look inland beyond which, somewhere in the wet wilds 2824 miles distant, is the Bay of Fundy (highest tidal rise and fall in the world). Cardiff, of course, is holder of the record for the second highest rise and fall, a claim I've at times seen challenged by both Newport and Barry and I seem to recall Porthcawl having a go too.

Exit from the park is via the gate at its lower end to follow Bradford Place on to The Kymin and its grounds. The path through here leads down to the sea. The Kymin, a grand house currently used by the Council for leisure activities and meetings, is the oldest structure in Penarth dating from 1710. You can get married here and afterwards, according to Council promotional literature, play petanque in the grounds.

We reach the front, the Esplanade, at the same time as a rush of walking pole outfitted pensioners on a coast ramble. For a moment the way to the 1894 art deco pier is blocked by an excited fuzz of coloured waterproof, rucksack and map-hung grey hairs working out which way next. John and I take tea inside in the tea shop just beyond the tai chi class and the twirly selling guide books. The sea washes all the way from here to Newfoundland. Cardiff? Not Cardiff at all.

Return is ten minutes up the hill through Alexandra Park to Penarth rail station and a Sprinter back to Cardiff Central.

Varini's *Three Ellipses for Three Locks*

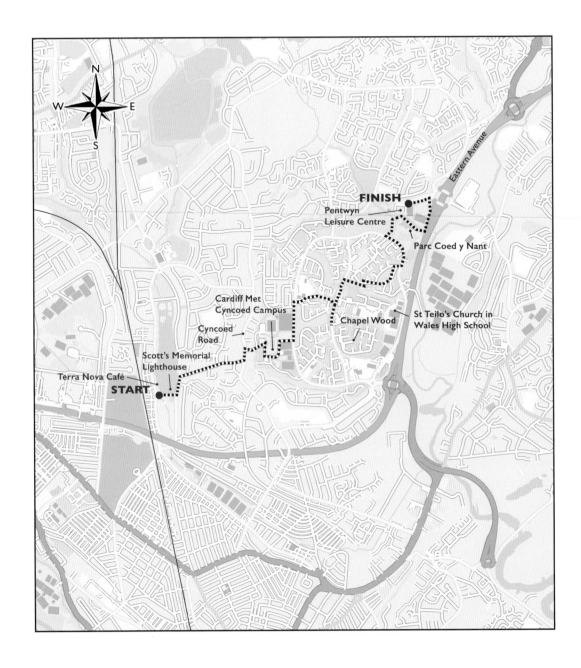

14. ROATH PARK LAKE TO
   PARC COED Y NANT

A linear walk from the lake prom of one of Cardiff's oldest parks to the lake prom of one of its more recent. This is initially a hill walk, climbing Penylan before crossing the Cardiff Met Campus to ramble down through the little visited (unless you live there) trees and terraces of the Llanedeyrn Estate. Finish is at Pentwyn Leisure Centre.

Start: Lake Road West gate of Roath Park Lake
Finish: Pentwyn Leisure Centre
Distance: 2.99 miles
Initial hill climb then steadily downhill. 28 bus from city centre to Lake Road West. Return on 58 bus from Pentwyn Leisure Centre

www.plotaroute.com/route/524380

I start with tea in the Terra Nova Café just down from the gate before proceeding to the prom itself. Promenading is a civilised practise. It needs to be done slowly, be full of talk with companions, ice cream or cigar in hand, walking stick, well-shined shoes, drifting down Las Ramblas, across the Promenade des Anglais, along the railinged front of Victorian Penarth. Roath Park Lake's version is along the top of the dam formed from the excavations made here when the park was first constructed. A half mile long lake was created where there was once a meandering stream and fields of unproductive bogland.

At weekends and in summer the lines of benches are all occupied, pushchairs, wheelchairs, kids' scooters, bread in bakery quantity thrown waterwards by all-comers. Scott's memorial lighthouse, which is not a house and has no light, is the unvisitable centrepiece. I skirt the toilets (closed) and the spot where, in season, the ice cream van gets parked. Summer sales are better here than anywhere else in Cardiff. Beyond is the site of the vanished changing rooms and the now dismantled diving platform.

This lake, almost called Lady Bute's Lake, opened on land donated by the Third Marquis in 1894. Not all that altruistically it turns out. With Bute things often weren't. Once the lake was in place he built a line of grand houses to overlook it. Property, then as now, increases in value the nearer it is to

the sight of water. Initially lake swimming was enthusiastically enjoyed by the local population. But those pollution-free days vanished as the century progressed and fast buck eager builders misconnected sewage pipes to landfall drains. Upstream, on land much nearer the Cardiff atomic bomb maker in Llanishen, alleged leakages were claimed to have given the lake fish three eyes. Bathers went elsewhere.

I climb steep Cefn Coed Road passing any number of majestic mansions and set back residences, castellations, towers, red brick outbuildings, gardens that roll back for miles. The air is full of the sound of motorised hedge clippers as a small army of green ripstop-clad gardeners cut back a summer's growth from the districts pre-eminent hedge – the laurel.

Towards its top the hill is clustered with parked cars on both sides, crushing pavements and blocking access. Student-owned, mainly, by attendees of Cardiff Met. This is a bone of much local contention with regular stand-offs between residents who want double yellow plus residents only, and a resistant Council who don't. Plans by the

On Cefn Coed Road

Gates at Cardiff Met

University to significantly expand the size of their campus have so far failed but in this, Wales' university capital, it's only a matter of time.

I cut across the campus to access Llanederyn. If the gates were locked then I'd need to divert. I'd backtrack along Cyncoed Road to reach the estate along Circle Way West, a name that resonates not with the land's history but its dissonant Brave New World future. But locked the gates rarely are. The City's 52 bus has its terminus inside and there are acres of car park although, to judge by the insidiousness of Met-operated meters and the prevalence of warning signs against transgression, you can see why student attendees leave their run-abouts on Cefn Coed.

The campus is large and is set right on the border between landed-gentry Cyncoed and socially housed Llanedeyrn. Cardiff Met has its schools of education and sport here. The campus is a city within a city, a futuristic-looking containment of blue astro-turf pitches and big box gyms. Everyone I see seems to be wearing shorts or trackies and proceeding at a jog. This is not heart attack central. That's further on in estate land where smoking is *de rigeur* and supersize a constant measure.

Llanedeyrn is named after sixth century Saint Edeyrn who, in the company of fellow desperado Isan, set about converting local pagans to the one true faith. They started at Llanishen before moving across to the village subsequently named Llanedeyrn. Edeyrn's church or, at least, the building that it eventually became, still stands at the side of Eastern Avenue.

Construction of the Llanedeyrn Estate began in the late 60s, social housing for the less well-off and those displaced by town centre slum clearance. 3500 homes were built for an expected population of 12,000. The land was gradually sloping farm liberally splashed with woodland. In the build the farms went but many stretches of wood were retained. The plan was to create inexpensive terraces and low-rise blocks separated with wood and path. Roads would circle but not cross, access would be along path and subway. On the gentle slopes of Llwyn y Grant and Coed y Gorse would be made a utopia for the many: school, clinics, an integral shopping centre, new pubs, a community centre, green open space and copious tree-filled air.

The sub-estates that comprised the district, all fifteen of them, retained the names of the woodland and fields they displaced. Pennsylvania, Wellwood, Springwood, Chapelwood, Wern Goch. I track down through signposted Pennsylvania looking hard for the US connection but not finding it. No wonder. Sylvania is Latin for woodland. Calling it Penn's Woods would have been much more prosaic. Road turns to path, run with men walking dogs and boys on wheelie-spinning bikes, nobody talking, and as expected everyone smoking.

The path takes me over a concrete footbridge crossing the Estate's central Llanedeyrn Drive. Maelfa, Llanedeyrn's slowly beating heart, a tower block with a fractured and poorly lit shopping mall at its base. Described as a "problem" by the council it is being unhurriedly rebuilt when I arrive and, no doubt, completed by the time you do. Outside are the bright yellow and red orange checkerboard walls of the Council-managed community centre. This is naturally known as the Hyb. Free Wi-Fi, into work help, library, café. Councils doing what they should.

Further south are the four bedroom depths of Roundwood where the properties overlook each other and everyone knows where you are, where you've put your keys, how expensive your tv is, if you are in bed, if you've locked your car. Unsafe and unsure, a place with a postcode that puts it top of Wales' list for burglaries. Yet all is calm as I pass with not a wrecked car or boarded window out of place.

My route on is through what were once the edges of Chapel Wood with much of the treescape still in place. Lines of terrace peep through leaf cover, a touch of abandoned furniture and lager can but you can see much the same in Rumney or Heath. A now privately-owned council house has been improved with a new breeze-block and oak-fence frontage, terraced front garden and proud marble nameplate – Castell Curl, Curl's Castle. Indeed.

I reach Circle Way again, East this time. Go round this roadway fast enough and you'll catch sight of yourself up ahead. But you couldn't, it's too full of humps and chicanes. If I went right I'd skirt the edge of St Teilo's Church in Wales High School. This has been built, appropriately for a church school, right on top of Chapel Wood's vanished since the sixteenth century Llanforda Chapel, and where the ancient graveyard was. The dead, whoever those lost souls were, are now pressed into service as car park foundation and underpinning for walls.

Instead I go left to get to Parc Coed Y Nant which, with its long scrub slopes is about as different from the gentility of Roath Park Lake as you can get. The lake at its centre has been formed on bogland by diverting water from the nearby Nant Glandulas. There are fishing platforms but no fishermen. Dogs are walked and, it seems to me, at a slightly faster rate than they are in more relaxed Roath Park. Here there are no flower borders. No flowers actually and, now I'm looking, no bushes either. The Prom is tiny but there are ducks and there's a single glowing white swan. No one is currently throwing bread but the birds remain hopeful.

I walk the short distance on through the park to reach Pentwyn Leisure Centre. There was a functioning café here in the long past. Today all that's on offer is cold coke from a shiny machine. I sup mine and watch the swimmers in their warmed chlorine waters. Warmer here than outside among the endless green where it has now started to rain.

Return to Cardiff City Centre is on the 58 immediately outside.

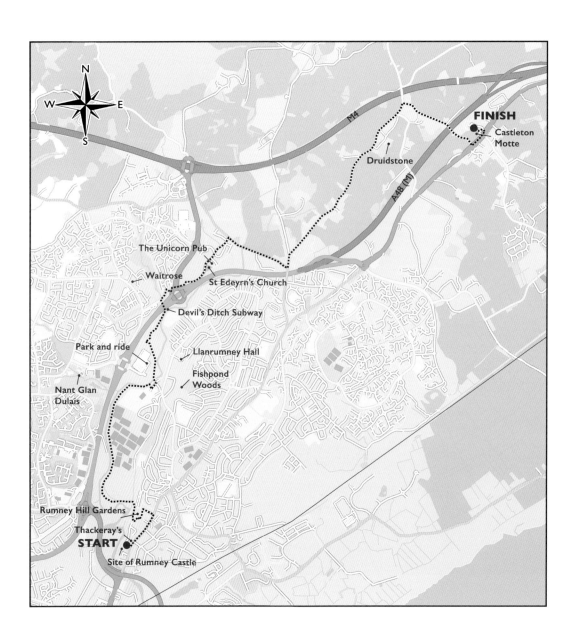

FINISH

Castleton
Motte

M4

Druidstone

A48 (M)

The Unicorn Pub

Waitrose

St Edeyrn's Church

Devil's Ditch Subway

Park and ride

Llanrumney Hall

Fishpond
Woods

Nant Glan
Dulais

Rumney Hill Gardens

Thackeray's

START

Site of Rumney Castle

15. RUMNEY CASTLE TO CASTLETON

A river valley walk north east out of Cardiff visiting the sites of castles, ancient churches, modern housing estates, river crossings and standing stones.

Start: Thackeray pub on Rumney Hill, a hundred yards up from the Pottery
Finish: Castleton Motte
Distance: 5.99 miles
Steep path down into river valley. Buses to the Pottery include 30, 45, 49, 50, 65, 815, 821, 823, X5 and X45. Return buses from Castleton – 30, X5

www.plotaroute.com/map/597125

In Cardiff valleys are a rare thing. The ones that made us famous are to the north, hidden by Caerphilly Mountain, languishing in the once industrial Wales of coal and terrace. But there is one that actually reaches us. This is the flat-bottomed vee of the River Rhymney, a watercourse that snakes its green sides across the eastern city. On the way it is joined by the veins and arteries of its many tributaries to bend in gouts of shining mud right into the Severn Estuary.

Given the Rhymney's propensity to flood and the need for the low-lying city to be protected from threatening waters the valley here has largely not been built on. It runs in an emerald arm back into the rising grounds of Cardiff north east: Pontprennau, Churchlands, Lisvane, Cefn Mably, lands of new flourishing as Cardiff gets its act together fulfilling its housing quota. 41,000 new homes by 2026 it says in the Local Development Plan.

John and I meet at the site of the castle that once guarded this valley. And as things often are in the island of Britain it is now a phantom with not so much as a single worked stone or mark on the earth to show where it stood. Sure, the street sign calls this Castle Rise and we've passed both Castle Avenue and Castle Crescent on the way up but of the stone redoubt itself there's not a trace. I unfold a scan of historian Allen Hambly's site drawing[22]. The houses of The Moat (into which Castle Rise has morphed itself) ran across Rumney Castle's width.

This was a Norman defensive structure, built as a ringwork soon after the invasion and later converted into a fortified

Castellations on Rumney Hill

manor house. As a centre of invader oppression it was largely destroyed in Madog ap Llywelyn's revolt of 1294. What was left just faded. Stones stolen for new builds, the bailey used to keep farm animals. The site was investigated by the Glamorgan and Gwent Archaeological Trust between 1978 and 1981 but their impressive results were then lost in a fire at the Trust premises in 1983. The site was formally scheduled to provide land for building in 1986 and that was that. Such is the fate of the past. Fade, fade, burn and burn.

Thackeray's, the quill pen signed pub here, was once known as Morgan's and before that as the Oaklands Hotel. Part of the castle crossed its car park. There's no Cardiff connection that I know of with the great Victorian writer but as a name it sounds good. Across Newport Road, spotted as we leave, is number 654, an art and crafts sloping red tiled house with a castellated tower added. Rumney Castle, Cae Castell[23], gone but still resonating.

A little up the hill Rumney Hill Gardens occupy land formerly set aside for a cemetery, in fact the brick building at the park's entrance was going to be the graveyard's mortuary. But priorities shift. Instead there are prize winning flower beds, tennis courts and a bowling green. It's early. There are no bench sitters, not yet. A path leads on into the valley. It should be a swift descent but John photographs every tree.

The valley revealed is a wonder, the Rhymney snaking in full oxbow loops across the floodplain. Reeds are stacked at bank side like corn. We are facing Llanedeyrn with its Maelfa Shopping Centre, the highest rise for miles. Behind

and above us now, watching the quiet valley, are the serried socialist windows of the Lynmouth Crescent Flats.

The path, hard topped here, is on a bund which protects the green expanse and its distant sports fields from constant inundation. This is dog walker territory. Wellingtons, Rohans, worn anoraks, knitted coats. The walkers compete for how many dogs they bring. A woman with five Scotties is outdone by the eleven-dog owner from the greyhound sanctuary. "Elderly and abused dogs," she tells me. "I save them all."

The council have turned much of this section of our route into a circular self-guided walk. The Rhymney Trail. This means the path will be in good repair and it should prove difficult to get lost. But then again. We go south of the university rugby pitches with Fishpond Woods in the distance. The woods are named after an actual fish pond once maintained by the owner of nearby Elizabethan Llanrumney Hall. Full of myth and Area 51 suspicion, that haunted place. It was owned by Sir Henry Morgan, the pirate. The headless corpse of Llewelyn the Last is buried in its walls. Ghosts wander its corridors. Gold coins chink in the ancient mortar. The same man who refurbished Thackeray's now owns it. We can expect great things.

Ball Lane reaches the river here and there's a pedestrian bridge, triple protected with menacing welded steel bars against crossing on motorbike but still totally accessible to BMX wheelie rollers who pass without concern. This bridge was originally a fragile wooden-plank affair, held to the banks by ropes, a swaying peril to anyone who used it. It led across two fields to Morgan's Tea Gardens on Llanedeyrn Road. These 1950s Tea Gardens operated from a wooden shack and sold cakes, cider, hot drinks and crisps. The site is subsumed today by Cardiff East Park and Ride, a double security-fenced car park cum bus station in which the council also store wheelie bins.

The Rhymney flows at speed. Shopping trolley. Burnt wood detritus. Bag plastic on the bushes. A birthday balloon in the branches. Scrap and junk. Graffiti in the very air. Traditionally it was the boundary between Glamorgan and Monmouth, the river curving thirty sinuous miles to its source in the southern Beacons. The outfall from the stream running through Parc Coed Y Nant is here as is Nant Glan Dulais which crosses Cardiff Golf Club on its way south from Lisvane.

A woman in her fifties out walking stops John and tells him a rambling tale about the railway that ran on the top of this causeway all the way down from Risca. "Carrying coal," she insists. "We'd go in the river to rescue lumps that fell off." Amazing. A whole industrial railway that somehow I'd missed. John and I check the bank's alignment and look for memorabilia. Sleepers. Rusted bolts. But there's nothing. And when I get home no mention of this fantasy in the official railway histories either.

Beyond Park and Ride we pass the end of a much decorated with community art subway known locally as Devil's Ditch. This runs under Eastern Avenue to surface in Pentwyn. It is covered with official graffiti done with great splashes of colour to depict a multi-racial mix of cartoon figures standing in front of an articulated lorry emblazoned with the words Respect and *Local Police*. Some of the cartoon figures wear police helmets. The mural has then been over-graffitied with the words 'The rich and the powerful piss on us daily and the media tell us its raining… The system isnt on your side….x' I smiled at the clarity of language and then thrilled at the kiss at the end. Mass literacy works, sometimes.

Here I make my first mistake. As walk planner and chief guide I insist on not taking the subway but continuing along the river bank. The path is there on the map but as we progress it degrades before us into swamp and slide. It thins and fills with pooled mud. It is overgrown with bramble the thickness of my arm. Tendrils rip. Branch traps catch our boots and bite us down. Triffids edge from every side. We get through, just.

There's now a second subway. This one is wrecked and super-graffitied in an extreme I thought we'd outlawed from Cardiff, and indeed, from the civilized west. Bust, broken and blasted with an overflow of illegible bile and un-fathomable vitriol. At its far end a path climbs to a stone stile at the south end of St Edeyrn's Church.

We are covered in mud and fragments of plant debris. John has boots filled with brown slush. I have a radiantly red scratch across the top of my head. We look perfect for tea and sandwiches at Waitrose, just up the road, which is where we go.

If you are using this book to guide you then don't come this way. Take the safer path. Go through the first subway where the community murals shine and the Nant Pontprennau passes in a gully. Turn right up the hill to cross the far edge of the Pentwyn interchange. Take the lane opposite and end up in to exactly where we are now, St Edeyrn's Church.

The Church had a starring role in *Gavin & Stacey* but is most famous for having that white painted square tower seen by anyone and everyone arriving in Cardiff via the A48M. St Edeyrn, who built the original church in the sixth century, is reputedly buried in the churchyard. The Church itself is believably medieval with low lintled doors and a sundial high up on the side of the tower.

I want silence but there's little. The trunk road continues to roar while all around me diggers are at work building another thousand or so houses to add to Cardiff's target. I always knew calling that other north of Penylan slab of 60s social housing Llanedeyrn was a mistake. This place is the real Llanedeyrn but on the sales boards, of course, it's known as something else. St Edeyrns Village. No apostrophe, it slows down sales.

The road on runs through new house heartland. Classy Persimmon, who also brand the larger district as Old St Mellons, promise a landscaped riverside park, an orchard, allotments and a new primary. The styles of houses offered are called things like the Alnwick, the Chedworth, the Hatfield, the Lumley, the Morden and the Moseley. Someone with a real sense of place has been hard at it thinking these up.

The Unicorn pub, once a depth of the country destination, stands boarded and closed as we pass, still looking for someone new to take it on. Beyond are fields, green, for now. A group of locals are out training their dogs. They blow high pitched whistles and yell but Jacko and Fudge, a quarter of a mile away foraging among the distant bushes, clearly don't want to return just yet.

Bridge Road rolls down to where Old St Mellons originally stopped before Persimmon extended it. There's a bilingual welcome sign and a celebration, still as fresh as the day it went up, of the district winning a Keep Wales Tidy Award in 2002. This slice of Old St Mellons works hard at maintaining its village atmosphere. The Community Council has erected interpretation boards and created historic trails. But the new build will soon drown it all.

Ahead the roads fork at the imposing and stone dog guarded gates of Marleigh Lodge. A Union Jack hangs limp on its garden flagpole. This is Druidstone Road, the Roman track out of Tamium (as Cardiff was then known), straight as a Roman die. It runs for a good mile and we need to walk single file for much of it to avoid the Porsches, Mercs and high-end BMWs that pass. This place is also known by some as Millionaire's Row, the site of some of the most expensive houses in Cardiff. Check the names: Richmond, Little Acre, High Trees, Doric House, Longueville Court, The Limes, The Orchard, The Manor. If it were not for the occasional Bron y Coed you'd think you were in the Home Counties. As far as the mansions themselves are concerned there's not a lot to glimpse. The fences, walls and great Leylandii hedges keep the world at bay.

Up beyond Pen Deri the habitations end and the ploughed fields commence. This is also where Cardiff finishes and Newport begins although untypically there's no Newport sign welcoming visitors. We just amble in.

Of the druids we have so far found no trace but the stone after which this ancient route was named still stands. In the garden of Druidstone House, on private land and behind banks of trees, this fat female stone sits and radiates. It's about five feet tall and the same in width, a replica of Maen Llia in the Brecon Beacons. Its magnetic majesty, however, is severely compromised by the outbuildings erected behind it and the double fence to its immediate front. To keep the stone in or visitors out? At night it doubtlessly shifts and spins signalling to the aliens who erected it and curing the Gaia earth's ills.

After 1.4 miles Druid-stone Road finally gives up. Around we can hear the traffic on the M4 and the A48M, both flushing through in their cuttings. We follow Coal Pit Lane south. This turns out to be a mistake. The traffic here is zoomingly impossible. The alternative cross field foot-path is perfectly manageable, if slightly overgrown, and only a little longer.

The Druidstone

Where Coal Pit crosses Eastern Avenue John stops to photograph a set of horse heads and other equinine knick knackery embedded in a house wall. Amid a flurry door-banging, dog barking, and engine roaring the vest-wearing owners suddenly exit their property in a battered pickup. Through a wound-down window they demand to know what John is doing. "I'm photographing these knick-knacks," he replies. There is indrawn breath. "Knick-knacks? We can't have you photographing our knick-knacks. Why don't you photograph the house instead? Stand over there and you can get it all in." A hand gestures from the cab. "But watch out for the dogs." John takes the indicated shot. Honour somehow preserved the owners drive off.

Across the field to our left, a few hundred yards further on, we can see it. An overgrown mound. Another great Norman motte. The castle that made Castleton. To reach it we follow Coal Pit Lane to its intersection with Newport Road. This is the Castleton most travellers see. But the place is not doing well. Litter blows. There are no shops. The B&B is up for sale. The 1816 Castleton Baptist Church with its great circular window is closed. The Baptist fellowship have gone.

The current name of this habitation is, of course, incorrect. This castle at our walk's end was known as Wentloog when it was built but the name didn't stick. What remains, which isn't much, sits hemmed in by a housing development. We walk up Mill Lane and then Wentloog Rise to find the motte comprehensively fenced in with 'Keep Out unsafe!' handmade notices pinned to the palings.

It's typically steep sided and at least 18 feet high with a 40 foot diameter top. Someone has carved an access path on the motte's south aspect but it's gated. There's a run wild garden on top. Seats, flower beds, shrubs. Indignity full on.

The Cotswold Archaeological Trust did a comprehensive assessment of the monument in 1997 and identified the site as the principal stronghold of the Gwynllwg lordship. There are records that show it was built by the de Nerbers family and then burnt down by Owain Glyndwr in 1402. Later castle-like stone structures, possibly the remains of the medieval chapel of St James, still cluster the eastern side of the motte's base. But as an antiquarian attraction it's pretty hopeless, blocked in, overgrown, degraded.

Is Castleton with its extant remains more atmospheric than Rumney where there's nothing? I'm not sure.

The bus back is from World War II memorial shelter across the road, the gift of Sir Leighton and Lady Seager of Bryn Ivor Hall. Service is on the 30 or the X5. The latter winds at speed through most of far eastern Cardiff so expect

extensive suburban views. Its stop at the end of New Road is about 100 metres from where we set out. A full circle. Psychogeographers like that.

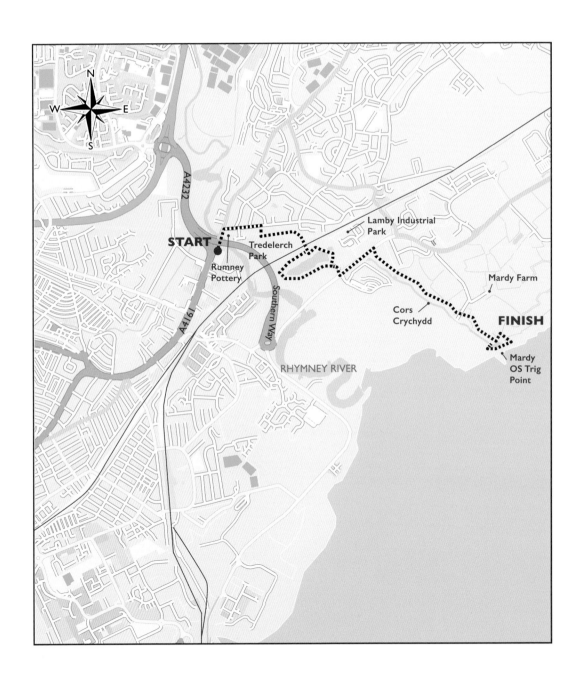

16. LAMBIES

A circular walk from the 400 year old pottery at the Rhymney River's edge, through the new Tredelerch Parc and around its lake to cross the Lamby flatlands to the sea wall, reach the trig point, and view the Estuary beyond.

Start and finish: Rumney Pottery
Distance 4.15 miles.
No inclines. Return buses to Cardiff Centre: 44, 49, 65 from The Potteries; 30,44,45,45B,49,50,65,65A,613,X45, X59 from nearby Ipswich Road

www.plotaroute.com/route/679802

East of the city at the coast's edge and running out the whole ten miles to our nearest neighbour, Newport, is one of Cardiff's least celebrated districts. The Lambies: a man-made landscape that more resembles the East Anglian Fenlands than it does any part of Wales. *Lambies* comes from *Langby,* a Viking name meaning long village, a place on the lowlands around the Rhymney estuary. More formally these ditch-drained, below sea-level marshes are known as the Wentloog Levels and are not really part of Cardiff, not that much of them anyway. The capital's administrative reach runs only as far as Broadstreet Common, a little to the east. Beyond, in what ought to be a greenbelt but isn't quite, Newport lays claim and its lion-faced yellow-winged dragon dominates all.

No urban explorer of the south Wales conurbations should be without at least one trek across these strange lands. The Romans were the first to drain them, followed by the Normans. In 1884 the Monmouthshire Commissioners of Sewers were in charge. Today they are maintained by Natural Resources Wales who build ever higher sea walls and deeper drainage ditches. Reens is the local name for these ditches, Rhynes over the water in Somerset. Rhines in Gloucestershire. Rhewyn in Welsh.

"To be completely lost is a good thing on a walk" wrote Tom Clark in his masterpiece *In Praise of Walking*, which I've recently read again. I'd been with Tom at a festival in Cornwall and wanted to remind myself how good a poet he is. But we are not going to get lost today, not down here so near to the city and the sea.

The walk starts at Rumney Pottery, bottom of Rumney Hill. The pottery itself stands where the Romans had their river crossing. There was once a quay here. Fishing henges. Clusters of huts. The potter's clay came from local fields. The present pottery building is eighteenth century and there's talk about parts being earlier than that.

Robert Giles, the Rumney Potter

Robert Giles, the current potter was the last to dig clay from the riverside. "People want finer materials now. China clays. We've had to switch." His family have been potters here for at least seven generations. 400 years of crock making and still in action. The pottery specialises in commemorative plates and mugs. Pontypridd Golf Club Centenary. Barry Dock Lifeboat 1901-2001. Mount Pleasant Presbyterian Church 1885-2010. I buy a Barry Dock RNLI mug as a souvenir. John snaps Robert Giles posing.

We follow the post-war houses that line New Road to access Tredelerch Parc via an avenue of dark trees. This is fronted by a trio of graffitied no horse-riding no golf balls notices and a set of industrial-strength bike barriers. Sets the tone. The park is wide and deeply green, recently mowed with a traversable path cut by sit-on machines across its centre.

The main rail line is crossed by footbridge at the end of Brachdy Lane. A lone pony watches us as we go. Strategically placed signage continues. The whole world is literate now. Here notices against trespass emerge from the greenery to warn of DNA Advanced Forensic Marking. We know you by your sweat and your touch. Come in here and we'll get you. We stick to the official path.

The footbridge to Tredelerch Lake

The footbridge gives immediate access to the recently created (2003) Tredelerch Lake. Earlier this stretch of freshwater was one of the bulbous ox-bow bendings of the river, all sink mud and gleaming slime. Today it's smooth and duck-filled. Swans glide. Fishermen sit in meditation, rods pointing out towards satori. We clip the lake's edge absorbing the feel-good negative ions that water always gives as we go. The path bends across a curving and reed-edged board walk and then drops us onto the Lamby Way roundabout. High speed vehicular rant, roar and rasp. An open-windowed coupé blaring monster rap and driven by two partying women of a certain age almost catches my boot.

Parc Tredelerch, Rumney

Cors Crychydd reen

We head east, along what is now also the route of the Wales Coast Path. It takes us a few hundred metres through the banging dust of over-trafficked Lamby Way before turning seawards through a waymarked gate to pass along the eastern edge of the still active Cardiff Council Lamby Way refuse tip. In the distance trucks disgorge and black-bagged waste is raked and flattened. Protecting us from these horrors is Cors Crychydd (Heron's Marsh), the Council's new 'mitigation' reen, named by the locals the Council claims although this feels slightly unlikely. It's wider than most drainage ditches, breadth enough to send a barge down. Geese and duck today.

The reen path runs all the way to sea across an entirely flat land. East are Sea Bank and Mardy Farms along with a run of caravan and car dismantling businesses at the edge of hidden by bush Lamby Industrial Park. The business there is a mixture of boiler plant maintenance, taxi offices, aluminium bashing, fire extinguisher supply, air vent installation, office furniture and security guarding. But on the path it's all berry picking, nature watching, sun bathing, and cloud gazing, a green calm with pond skaters and dragonfly. Up front the sea wall rises and there upon it is the trig.

There is a whole sub-culture surrounding the Ordnance Survey's trig points. There are spotters and number collectors. Societies of runners who rush between them, explorers who navigate to them using only the reference numbers from maps, fanatics hell bent on visiting every single one. The

The Mardy trig point

Mardy example is squat and, like many, has seen better days. It's RT232776 for collectors. From it you can view Dial Hill in Clevedon (ST407719) and Middle Hope at Sand Bay (ST327660). No doubt, like the Mardy trig, they too have had their metal numbers stolen by collectors.

We stare out at the receded tide and the great flat expanse of the gleaming Severn Estuary, Rhymney River subsumed, sight lines clear to a flat watery horizon.

The sensible route, and indeed the plan, is to return now the way we came. More or less. Take the trail on the reen's western side back to Tredelerch Lake, route round that patch of smooth water's as yet unwalked southern edge to reach the Pottery again. Either that or cross east via Maerdy Lane to skirt Lamby Industrial Park experiencing the utter contrast of activity available in these flatlands and then emerge at the Lake's south east corner and return from there. We haven't decided which but either would work. An easy stroll. These are the routes that *Walking Cardiff* recommends and the ones users should take.

But I want to have just a small look at the Rhymney River's estuary edge and climb the sea wall to walk its bund-top path a little way west. Below us are the dark and faintly steaming mounds of Cardiff city compost, the results of green bin collecting and the decomposed cut excesses from the city's parks. They are pushed about by tractors and turned by machines, shoved through tubular filters, transformed into something a gardener would desire. Beyond the fence and smoking outside the Portacabin an official in white shirt and decent trousers stands talking on his phone.

I hail and ask how far the path I'm on goes. "Right the way round." "Can I get back to the road this way?" "Yes." "I won't find myself sliding into the river?" "Certainly not." The naivety of it all is that instead of believing my utterly reliable OS Mapping phone app I listen to this gush.

Initially the walking is splendid. Great sea views across flat water to the islands. Slowly rotting groynes strut out in long lines across the mud. Tata Steel's plant is in the Cardiff distance. The path is clear, level, and purposeful. But all that soon changes. After a few hundred metres we reach the place where East Creek once leaked into the sea. Its estuary mouth is now a beach. It has the expected tide-line detritus mash of brick, bust mortar and sea worn plastic, but it also has sand. The genuine article. Browny-yellow. A good 25m stretch, enough to leave a line of boot prints in as if this were an advert for Jamaican rum.

Beyond the beach the path becomes more an animal track in the overgrowth, before degenerating into pretty much nothing as we round the Rhymney's ever bending edge. Onwards? It's a gamble. I make it a rule that unless it is absolutely unavoidable never go back. At first it's okay. Ankle grass with mud and debris below, nothing sinking or sliding. Not much. The river in its slinky slime away to our left.

But as we plough ever more slowly through the distance the grass turns to rush, knee high, then thigh high, waist high and finally up to our chests. The river's edge is increasingly hard to see. There are foot traps, blunders, mis-steps, spills, ankle turners, and slides and slopes. The temperature and humidity rise steadily. It's a warm day anyway but round here the air is thick enough with damp to squeeze out drops. After at least an hour of this with multiple stops to fend exhaustion and to contemplate our future we reach a place from which we can see in the distance the Rhymney River Boat Club, a cluster of bank-lolling yachts and dinghies with floating walkways beached and bending out to them across the mud. Has to be good but turns out to be not. The river is between us. On our side is the impenetrable fence guarding the at this point capped Lamby Way rubbish dump. Plans to build a golf club on its top and to allow leisure access appear to have been shelved.

I work out a plan B. Is the razor wire-topped mesh fence penetrable? Could I get over it? If I phoned for help would they send a tractor? Could I call in a helicopter somehow?

Writer Rescued From Mud Adventure. *Walking Cardiff* a Failure say Seren Books. But we sweat on. For another hour. Eventually the reeds lessen, slightly, and a hole in the Dump fence appears. We take it. Doesn't matter where it goes. Anywhere to escape this river. On the far side is a proper track, big enough for vehicles, and then through greenery a second fence hole with moving vehicles on its far side. Lamby Way again in all its overexcited glory. It's been an adventure. Tom would have approved.

Over the road at this point is a path which runs to the western end of Tredelerch Lake. Just where we wanted to be. What I'd love right now would be a café stop but this new Cardiff parkland offers no such glories. In fact the whole district of Rumney, replete as it is with chip shops and hair

dressers, seems to lack a café culture. Nearest stop to where we are right now is M&S on Newport Road, shoppers in designer trainers and statement prints. A bridge too far. We stroll on, back to the Pottery. "There are walks in which we tread in the footsteps of others and walks on which we strike out entirely for ourselves," wrote Tom Clark. This one has been a slice of both.

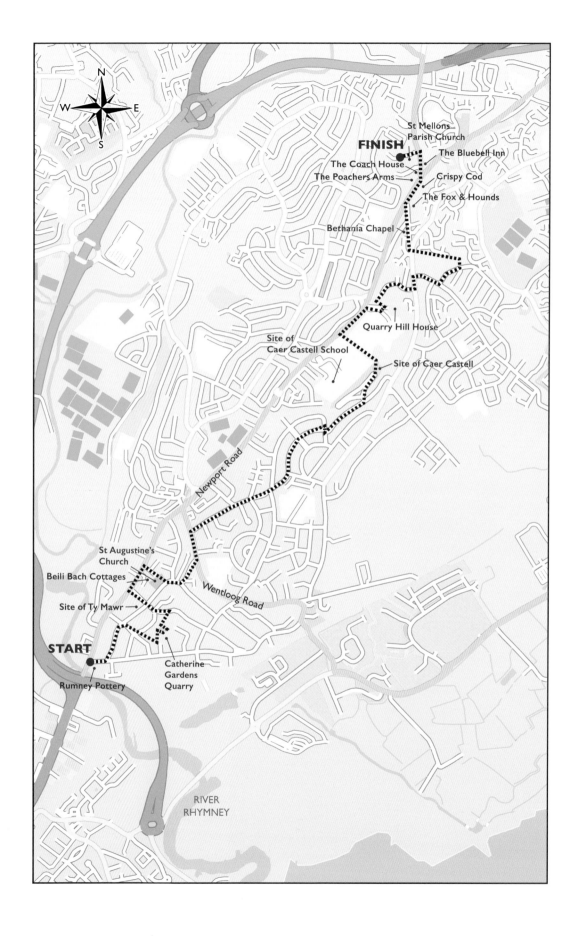

17. RHYMNEY BRIDGE TO ST MELLONS

A zig-zag from the bridge over the River Rhymney to the Parish Church of St Mellons atop its eminence to the east. The walk takes in abandoned quarries, sea vistas, pre-fab corrugated roofed semis, a little-known Norman motte, a Trowbridge skateboard park, constellations of chapels and pub clusters to finish in the centre of an old Monmouth village now forever cemented into the fabric of the capital city.

Start: Rhymney River Bridge
Finish: Just up from the chip shop in St Mellons
Distance: 3.55 miles
Some inclines but nothing too taxing. X45 or 30 buses out from the City Centre; return on the X45 or 30.

www.plotaroute.com/route/447927

You wonder why they all want to get through here in their cars and trucks and on their buses, everyone at the same time, pummelling the placidity out of the riverine air. It's 8.30 and before the sun gets up to blast us. John and I have started at the bridge over the River Rhymney again, Rumney Bridge as it's mistakenly called, the many times re-built crossing from Kairdiv to Rompney. This was once a border between two counties, when Rumney was part of Monmouth and held different allegiances. But in 1938 the district was incorporated into the City of Cardiff and all that changed.

Once a hamlet clustering around the Church of St Augustine near the top of the hill the district has done nothing but expand since industrial Cardiff adopted it as a residential outlier. To judge by the infill along most of its periphery that expansion hasn't finished yet.

For most of *Walking Cardiff* John and I have rejoiced in the as experienced by your calves' realisation that most of Cardiff is flat. And if not absolutely so then only with the most gradual of inclines. Rompney is the big exception, and how. Rumney Hill, the once fortified guardian of east Cardiff, has a gradient that makes cyclists get off and push. We avoid the hill by instead following New Road, a twentieth century hill-skirting creation across the lower Rompney farmland, to access Catherine Gardens off Ty Mawr Avenue. The Ty Mawr of that name, the big house, was Rumney Manor, remnants of which lasted until the 1930s. It stood at the junction of Ty Mawr Avenue and Ty Mawr Road.

Catherine Gardens, a landscaped green redoubt complete with a swings and slides play area, is actually a former building stone quarry. We scramble among the ferns and bramble overgrowth behind the long slide so that John can take shots of the industrial scar now almost completely lost under the green.

Catherine Gardens, Rumney

We exit up Ty Mawr Road to climb the hill. On top we take a lane next to number 716 Newport Road that unexpectedly lands us in the front drive of a short stubby row of ancient cottages. This is Beili Bach, at least 300 years old and was built as a single storey housebarn where the farmers shared their accommodation with their animals. Warm in winter and, in those days, no-one cared about the smells. At the left hand end is a stile into St Augustine's churchyard. 'God's Acre' as the church noticeboard calls it, noting an origin as far back as 1108. The tower complete with battlements, six bells and a clock that dates from the fifteenth century. Roofers are in action fixing the slates as we pass.

Beili bach, Rumney

The Rumney we are moving through was largely agricultural until the post-War Cardiff boom. Traces of that past keep appearing. At the top of Church Road at the end of a row of semis built in a variety of between the wars British domestic styles stands Whitehall, an eighteenth century farm house once owned by John Wood, a former Clerk to Cardiff Council. Through the half-opened window a notice advises visitors to 'Beware' but fails to say of what.

Ty Fry Road is an ancient byway that once passed orchards and fields to reach the Ty Fry great house. As we walk the district perceptibly changes from owner occupied to rented. Pre-fabs appear, BISF[24] steel framed system-built structures, two storey post-war palaces with corrugated iron roofs still keeping out the rain. Architectural wonders if you are a fan of estate construction. Just a house if you're not. The streets are named after Welsh seaside resorts – Manorbier, Rhyl, Penrhos, Rhossilly.

The indicators now all start to tell the same story. Furniture in front gardens. Mattresses stuffed between houses. Speed bumps. Overgrown privets. Letters missing from road signs: 'Rossill oa'. Giant artificial butterflies and ladybirds affixed to walls. The road rises to meet Caer Castell Place. The Bristol Channel is now visible with a view straight

across to Clevedon and the islands. The sight of a seascape in a port city should not be in the least unexpected but, somehow, it is. The sea when you least expect it. Not the sea at all, some argue, merely a big river.

The channel from Caer Castell Place

Castle Heights is an orange brick recent development. Near here is Caer Castell, a Roman camp as some maps have it but in reality a mightily overgrown Norman motte put up on the edge of marshy ground in order to watch across the water for raiders.

We cut along the fenced lane separating the now demolished Eastern High School from Catholic St Illtyd's. Easter High was my old stomping ground when it was Caer Castell Secondary Modern and I struggled my way through its brand new GCE-stream. The overgrown grass of the former rugby field is still as clear of trash as it was after I'd litterpicked it, in punishment for some teenage misdemeanour, in 1962.

The way south passes the site of Quarry Hill House. This was built by the civil engineer Joseph Benjamin Hemmingway in 1850, and now, like so many once great houses, does time as a care home. We follow a lane back down to Meadvale Road. Rumney is done and Trowbridge begun. Before us is a sweep of 1970s housing that runs all the way to new St Mellons.

This is a rougher land. The drought has burned the green brown and in the open spaces locals have set fire to tree stumps to complete the job, adding a certain city fringe glamour to it all. We head uphill passing an entirely empty skateboard and BMX park before emerging on Bethania Row. Old St Mellons. The distinction between the ancient village and its new brash and youth-bedevilled upstart neighbour is very clearly made. Noticeboards illustrating a district heritage walk are headed 'Old St Mellons Community Council' and, although the massed encroaching new construction might deny the reality, those who live here insist this is still a village.

On the Row itself stands Bethania, a Methodist Chapel from 1820, and across the road from it, tree-riddled and overgrown as if preparing itself for a gothic horror, is Bethania graveyard. The Fox and Hounds next door, originally a cottage and smithy, was turned into a pub in 1869 and has never looked back.

We cross Newport Road heading north. More pubs come into view. The Star, now renamed the Poachers Arms (no apostrophe), the Coach House, formerly the White Hart, then the Blue Bell Inn, still Blue, and offering 'Great Food Served All Day'. In the days when local authorities made up their own licencing laws this was a boundary. Cardiff pubs like the Fox and Hounds stopped tap at 10.30 while Monmouth drinkeries such as the Blue Bell rolled on until 11.00. Trains of drinkers nightly stumbled across the separating Ty'r Winch Road.

Traces of the long past remain in this innermost core of Old St Mellons. The Old Bakery is clearly labelled while the School House stands on the site of former Poor House. Up the hill is the long sloping graveyard of St Mellons Church. Here, outside the walls and in unhallowed ground, were discovered a great pile of human bones. Investigators ascribed these to the dead drowned in the great flood of 1607. They are now reburied inside beneath a plaque reading 'Here lie the remains of Christian Souls discovered in land next to this churchyard 15th November, 1997.' A sexton out collecting churchyard litter asks if we've seen it. One of the wonders of the Old St Mellons world.

Our destination, St Mellons Parish Church, hilltop site visible to travellers for miles in all directions, was founded in 1108. The Mellons name comes from either the sixth century Saint Melaine of Brittany or Mellonius, Bishop of Rouen in the fourth. One of them was born nearby but legend is unsure which. The village's Welsh name is Llaneirwg, the Llan (or holy site) of Saint Eurwg, a holy man from the Roman period. There's a slice of this historical conundrum on the hard to read Heritage Trail noticeboard outside. Dominating the graveyard is the snapped pillar memorial Joseph Benjamin Hemmingway.

Back on the main road the Crispy Cod Chip Shop for the famished isn't open yet while the Sea View Store for those who'd prefer a just Kit Kat certainly is. Chocolate in hand we catch the 30 bus rattling back to the centre. Outside the sky continues to glow.

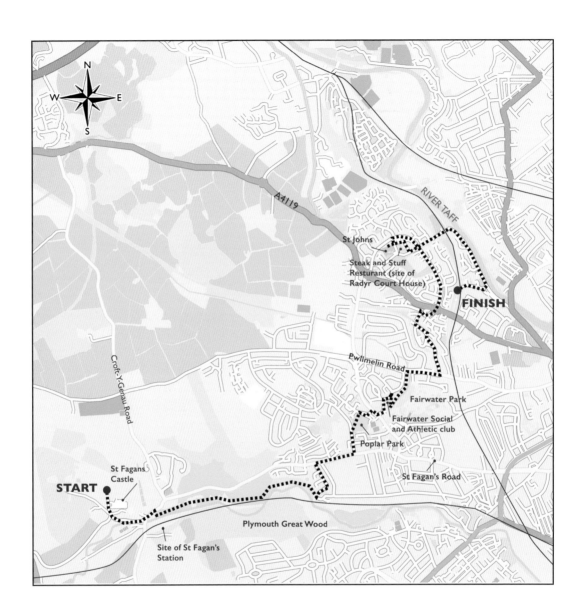

N
W   E
S

A4119

RIVER TAFF

St Johns

Steak and Stuff
Resturant (site of
Radyr Court House)

FINISH

Pwllmelin Road

Fairwater Park

Fairwater Social
and Athletic club

Croft-Y-Genau Road

Poplar Park

St Fagan's Road

St Fagans
Castle

START

Site of St Fagan's
Station

Plymouth Great Wood

18. ST FAGANS TO DANESCOURT

A walk from a great civil war battleground, along river valleys, through old and new estates, across parks known and unknown, to reach the burial place of Roald Dahl's family and then catch the train back home.

Start: St Fagans Car Park. 32A bus from Cardiff Central
Finish: Danescourt Rail Station
Distance: 4.52 miles. Return trains from Danescourt to Queen Street
Slight slopes and slow hills rather than steady climbs

www.plotaroute.com/route/613421

St Fagans is a land of myth and wonder. Always has been as long as I can remember and my memory goes right back. But it's closed when we get there. John and I meet in the car park where the name has changed. Welcome to St Fagans National Museum of History announces a bright new nameplate. The older brown direction sign points to The Museum of Welsh Life. It was the Folk Museum for most of my childhood. But who cares. Its assemblage of reconstructed buildings, everything from country churches to working-men's clubs, pigsties to Celtic camps, and terraced cottages to a soon functioning pub plus its unrivalled collections of harps, bardic chairs, hay rakes and a whole panoply of now vanished Welsh minutiae is dazzling. We will return and look another time.

John was out again last night at both the Ruperra and the Tredegar Arms so we take it slow. Not that any of our walks are ever really fast. A few paces along the dappled access lane gets us to the main Swansea-Cardiff rail line and the level crossing. It is down right now to let the nine o'clock Hitachi-built bi-mode IET pass. This deep GWR green and bullet-imitating piece of the world to come replaces the comfortable to sit on British 125s with an ironing-board seated foreign-designed future. The train does not take the strain as it once did. But it passes, nevertheless, in a suitably impressive rush before the gates rise and the cars roar again.

A wedge of land next to the track has been taken over by the Community Council as a local park. A noticeboard illustrated with musket-firing soldiers recalls the station that existed here and on to which Queen Victoria once alighted on her visit to St Fagans Castle. In 1648 there was also a great battle up the road[25] between rebel Parliamentarians and the roundhead New Model Army. 7500 men fought. 200 died. As it does around the sites of great battles the river ran red with their blood. Momentum won.

We climb Castle Hill passing still-thatched cottages with the high chimneys of St Fagans Castle rising behind them. If it wasn't for the traffic this could be the seventeenth century. To our right is the gate access to the Ely Trail, a path east following the river back into the built-up city. But as it enters its river valley the path descends into a road and rail-vanished green serenity. We could be in Radnorshire rather than the capital. The highway is up there beyond risen hedge but invisible. The rail line lost below. An occasional glimpsed green flash and suggestion of locomotive roar behind trees is all the evidence there is.

The Ely of the unexpected continues through glades rich in the scent of wild garlic. White flowers ripple below trees. Everything is bountiful or offers such prospects, this being spring and the weather fine. Then the whole sylvan shebang comes to an abrupt halt as housing appears between trees. There's a notice fixed to railings. All caps as such notices

usually are. 'I AM WATCHING – WHOEVER IT IS THAT KEEPS PUTTING THEIR DOG WASTE BAGS ON MY WALL – TAKE IT HOME AND PUT IT ON YOUR WALL! I WILL CATCH YOU!' It is almost worth hiding in the bushes to watch this suburban drama unfold. But we roll on. Up Glan Ely Close to reach St Fagans Road.

The housing stock here now we have climbed the slow hill to Fairwater often displays faux Elizabethan leanings. If we want comfort then the past always beckons. We take Gorse Place to access Poplar Park with its warning signs against Orse Riding, Motor Cycling and one, now completely upside down, against the hitting of golf balls. I ask a guy wearing two hearing aids which district are we in. "This is Fairwater," he says. "Where's Pentrebane?" "Up there," he points. In the distance. Somewhere. This will become a feature of the walk. Fairwater the all-encompassing. Pentrebane never to be discovered.

The houses here, in the still dappling sun, are in short terraces of fours and fives, climbing the hill in small staggers. Front gardens are optional. Communal grass bangs against low walls of grey concrete block. White painted handrails define sloping access paths. Parked cars are few, a sign of resident age or economic status or both. We track on, passing Fairwater Day Centre with its green mildewed nameplate and then the Social Club with its equally mould-covered sign advertising the availability of Worthington and Carling.

Near here once stood the grand mansions of Fairwater House and Fairwater Croft. Both owned by the illustrious and the great and both now long demolished, although Fairwater House lasted as an old people's home until 1994. The farmland around the great houses now forms Fairwater Park. Access is a lane just beyond the arbitrarily chosen brick and warning sign shambles that is the back of Fairwater Social and Athletic Club. Here the architect has abandoned form in favour of stickle brick and Duplo with exterior air-con units on every corner.

Fairwater Park is huge and hilly with the much vaunted, when it first opened, snowless ski centre on its southern edge. But we don't ski. We climb. Rolling on through endless Fairwater. The district took its name from the quality of the water springing in its wells. These were so good that today almost all have now been let into the sewer system.

North of the park, where Fairwater continues, the fifties housing is having its mains electricity renewed. Western Power are furiously digging trenches as if this were World War I. We pass vans advertising dog walking services and party planning, venue decoration and balloon supply. These are the new folk industries of the suburbs. North of Fairwater

Tandoori (which seems to be doing well) and the Dell-licious Sandwich Bar (now closed) housing blocks in the form of low-rise tenements face each other across green wedges of grass and small pathless parks. These are the new urban villages with quiet greens, stone lions on their gate posts and giant gnomes in their gardens.

Suddenly our winding road – Tangmere Drive – pitches us onto one of Llantrisant Road's many roundabouts. The frontier at last. Ahead is the new land of Danescourt. We Morris On.

As the name for a district Danescourt has plausibility although when you investigate it all falls apart. There were no Danes here. Just Radyr Court House and a now vanished mansion called Danesbrook House. It's Radyr really or, given the breadth and power of the lands we've just traversed, North Fairwater. It was created during one of Cardiff's successive booms in the mid-1970s, a huge estate of red brick and green boxes, determined to provide class enough to justify the shining new prices. The curving cul-de-sacs are named after local landowners (Matthew, Rachel, Lynch Blosse) or those connected with nearby Llandaff Cathedral (Urban, Pace, Pritchard, Seddon, Epstein and Rossetti). There's lots of grass. Verges and spreads.

We follow Danescourt Way as it curves into the district's ancient centre. Where Radyr Court stood, still stands in fact, 1469 newly painted onto its chimney. No longer a great house or quite the rambling pub with Indian restaurant upstairs that it became when the estate was developed in 1979. This is now a Steak and Stuff restaurant. Steak I understand. Stuff I'm not sure. There's a photo of the two new chefs looking slightly menacing in a case by the door.

Beyond is our destination, the graveyard of St John The Baptist's Church. Medieval origins hard to take, says John Newman's *The Buildings of Wales* (Penguin, 1995). He objects to the polychromatic crazy-paving of the walls. Five replica Celtic crosses. One of them belonging to the Dahls. Roald's family. In 1920 they were living in the now vanished Hogwarts-style Radyr farmhouse of Ty Mynydd. In the February Roald's older sister Astri died from appendicitis at just 7 years old. Harald, Roald's father, was heartbroken and died himself a month later. The two are buried here beneath the graveyard's most imposing of Celtic stones. Sofie Magdalene, Roald's mother, stayed the course to die in 1967. Her memorial is here too. It's a poignant moment standing in the long grass. Danescourt massed behind us. None of it here when the Dahls were.

We find the lane that is Radyr Court Road running downhill from the Church to parallel the Taff. Despite flood warnings new houses are everywhere. Llandaff North's Hailey Park is visible over the river. There's a route back up through Radyr Court Close to cross the black bridge and reach our destination, Danescourt railway station.

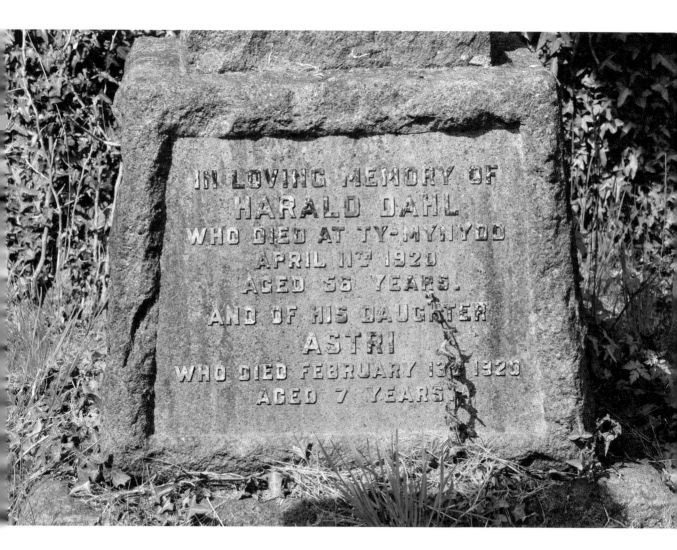

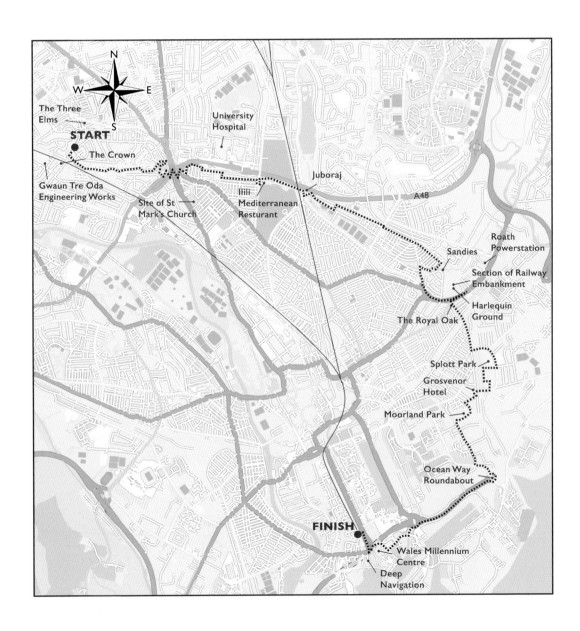

19. FOLLOWING THE ROATH BRANCH MINERAL RAILWAY

A walk following the now vanished Roath Branch of the Taff Vale Railway. This carried mineral trains from its junction with the main line south of Whitchurch Common to its terminus at Roath Dock sidings in the Bay. An easy and often downhill walk through some little-known streets hunting for the ghostly remains of industry. Definitely a walk for fans of trains.

Start: The Three Elms on Whitchurch Common 21/24/25 bus or on Heol Gabriel using the 35
Finish: Cardiff Bay railway station
Distance: 7.70 miles
Easy slowly downhill walk.

www.plotaroute.com/map/536273

I'm on the route following one of Cardiff's principal arteries that was, that is no more. In fact there's barely a trace. I am on the trail of the lost Roath Branch of the Taff Vale Railway. This line carried the city's black gold – coal from the Rhondda and the Aberdare valleys – and transported it to the sprawling Roath Dock. Here it was loaded via staithes and traverser hoists onto ships that reached the entire world. Cardiff, coal capital, engine of the empire, powerhouse of the globe.

The Roath Branch left the Taff Vale's mainline from the valleys to the city somewhere south of Whitchurch Common. It ran in a discrete arc for five miles to beach at the port's dock's where the coal trucks were stored in sprawling sidings. Empty ships queued to enter the docks, the West, the East, the Roath Dock and the Queen Alexandra. There was smoke and steam in the air, smells and clank and rattle. A train would traverse the downline every 30 minutes. They did that from the time of the branch's opening in 1888 to when it finally closed eighty years later. Trucks, waggons, boxes. Never a passenger and always hauled by steam. For the Roath Branch the diesels never arrived.

As an innovation the company ran a siding from where the track crossed the edge of the Harlequin Football Ground. This serviced Cardiff Corporation's coal-fed power station built to provide electricity for the new tram system. The tram depot on Newport Road was right next door. There were vast cooling towers at the end of Colchester Avenue. They dominated the skyline until the power station's demolition as uneconomic in 1972. Their fall was observed by half the city. The place where they stood is now the car park for Sainsbury's.

I've walked this route before, John in tow. That was in 2008 when I wanted something psychogeographic for *Real Cardiff*, a hunting for the lost and a pursuing of the vanished. And the route was that for sure. John had a film camera and only one roll of film. Twenty-four pictures were all he took. But this time we go digital where the shots never end. We begin where the rail points were, the Roath Branch's source, just off Whitchurch's College Road.

Access is on the 21/24/25 bus to the Three Elms where the poet John Tripp (see Walk 20) drank until he was banned. A short walk along College Road takes us to the rail junction's site just between the still extant Taff Terrace and the now demolished Crown Hotel. Behind stood the Gwaun Tre Oda Engineering Works. This was at one time operated by a Charles de Burgue, manufacturer of patent rail levellers. His company also made girders and crossbeams, significantly for Scotland's Tay Bridge, a fact we don't celebrate much in Wales. This Tay Bridge was the one that spectacularly fell down in 1879. It was celebrated by William McGonagall, known today as the worst poet in the English language.

Beautiful Railway Bridge of the Silv'ry Tay!
Alas! I am very sorry to say
That ninety lives have been taken away
On the last Sabbath day of 1879,
Which will be remember'd for a very long time.
A Welsh shame.

The junction sidings here were enormous, capable of holding more than 2240 wagons. They stretched from the Crown Hotel to the original and now demolished St Mark's Church[26] on the Gabalfa interchange. Today not a marker of any description remains. We walk down Coed Arian, a serpentine meander of recent houses, a secret Whitchurch that you only ever reach if it is your destination. Through roads don't exist. But a path does. At the end of Coed Arian a lane known as The Cut takes us through trees, across the grill under which the safely channelled Whitchurch Brook[27] roars, to reach Silver Birch Close, a further snake of new housing that stretches on to the northern reaches of Mynachdy.

In terms of size the sidings reached a crescendo where they've created Mynachdy Park. In today's low sun it's a brightly lit green expanse fringed with kids playpark, shrub and goal posts. It's an easy dive through the tunnels of the Gabalfa Interchange, passing the sort of graffiti[28] you might expect – "I Am The Revolution" – done in traditional style complete with tag and then something right on the new culture button – "Trans Rights Are Human Rights" – no tag, can of spray paint running out towards slogan's end.

The trains running from the sidings to the docks rattled with wagons from right across the south Wales coalfield – Cory Brothers, Ebbw Vale, Ocean, Welsh Navigation, Llanbradach, Welsh Associated Colliers, Nixon's of Abergorki, Tylacoch, Bwlfa, Mountain Ash and Merthyr Vale. In all their number, and through the many years they operated they must have left indelible traces. Smoke stains, steam burn, axel oil, rail sleepers, scatterings of track ballast and scurries of coal dust. The whole ceaseless detritus of a railway. But today it's all wiped away, buried, gone. Every last piece. The new Cardiff world is much purer and quieter place.

We skirt the bridge from the University Hospital to parallel the long allotments that grow beans and potatoes, cabbages and carrots all the way to the bottom of Clodien Avenue. These were the fields of Allensbank Farm. Below the Grape and Olive (now reborn and mightily refurbished as Ilili Mediterranean Halal Restaurant) the rail tracks ran along the bed of what is now Cardiff's dual carriageway M4 feeder, Eastern Avenue, the A48(M).

Here the Taff Vale Roath Branch crossed under the Rhymney Railway main line to Cardiff Queen Street. This track and its bridge over Wedal Road is still extant and still has trains running. But of the Roath Branch, can I find a sign? I check the rail bridge's balustrades and supporting stonework. There are a few blocks that could have been an embankment, in place when Roath Branch trains steamed. But in this psychogeographic ramble do they count as an actual railway relic?

Looping alongside the Juboraj restaurant in its very much post railway brick takes us to the long straight run paralleling Ty Draw Road. The Roath Branch steamed along the side of Penylan Hill in a cutting. A place of very slow and limited trainspotting (mostly 5700 class 0-6-0 pannier tankers although fanatics have claimed to have glimpsed train world exotics such as imported US war time locos and, on one occasion, a Deltic diesel derivative in all its glory but I'm not convinced). My old school friend Northmore and I sat here fifty years ago jotting down numbers. I thought this was a great experience but world-weary Northmore said it was a waste of time.

On this long walk down highways that were lanes when the Branch ran but are now roads with marketable names, the cutting has been comprehensively filled in. New housing sits in stubby-closes called Clos Derwen and Pant Yr Wyn. Further along is Boleyn Walk, a name with about as much local connection as Meghan Markle. The houses beyond it are called The Tudors. We take the lane behind them towards Waterloo Hill.

The tracks emerged from their cutting at the edge of the Sandies, a green space recently rebranded by National Resources Wales as Railway Gardens (how do these things happen?). The park has been extensively restructured as part of Natural Resources Wales' Roath Brook Flood Prevention Scheme. It's all flood banks and new plantings set out in an asymmetrical swirl. The Roath Branch had stubby sidings at this point leading to the power station, Cardiff Newport Road Goods Yard and Marcroft's wagon repair works.

The main track ran on an embankment to enable it to clear both Newport Road and the London main line. On the Sandies side was the Cardiff Harlequin Athletic Ground and a rope walk manufacturing ships' rigging. According to Daryl Leeworthy the ground was Cardiff's premier sporting place in the late Victorian period. Today's it is still very much in use in the hands of St Peter's RFC and strongly fenced against stray dogs.

Roath Branch bridge on Penylan Hill

For the pedantic, which we are, access is via the club house car park a hundred metres along Minster Road. Worth the trip, as it turns out, as the only significant railway relic of the entire branch stands here. An entire underpass tunnel complete with embankment balustrades and revetments stands with its tracks uprooted for scrap and its actual embankment largely demolished. Its ends have been bricked over and roller-shuttered to enable use as a car repair garage.

This remnant is best seen from the Harlequin Court side accessed via a desire path and bent out of shape fence paling. The legal route is back out via the club house and via super-busy Newport Road. This diversion two hundred metres up the main multi-lane highway takes us to where accommodation and reception for newly arrived refugees sit facing down a branch of Dunelm Mill. The Roath Branch crossed the road on a now vanished bridge to head dockwards along a great dyke that separated the CWS biscuit works (later Leo supermarket) from Pengam Moor. Both of those Cardiff features are gone to be replaced by housing, but the embankment remains.

We are south of the tracks now. This is where Roath ends and Splott begins. It's as true today as it ever was that in this city if you are deeply working class then you live south of that line formed by either the old Roman Portway (Newport Road, Cowbridge Road) or its fellow traveller, the main rail line. If you have aspirations then you'll live north. My mother doggedly insisted that this was always the case. But then she was wrong about a lot of things.

We pass the Royal Oak to walk up the slow slope of Beresford Road to reach the newly renovated in time for the arrival of electrification Beresford Bridge. Below us, visible from the far side, are the tracks of the London to Swansea main line. The local history society have been busy nearby installing plaques on both the Moorlands Hotel (1896-2004) and the site of the biscuit factory (1921-1970), now the Horwood Close estate.

Swinging left onto Muirton Road we dip under two rail bridges. One carries the still working main line link to the steel rolling plant while the other carried the lost Roath Branch. This is the first real sighting of what I was starting to think had become something even vaguer than a ghost, a phantom, trainspotter mist in the Cardiff air. Had the railway actually existed? This bridge says it did.

Roath Branch bridge, Splott

On the other side is the northern end of Splott Park, a great expanse of largely treeless green with dotted seagulls built on Pengam Farm land. In its centre where the open air baths were stands yet another council-run community Hyb. This is the word of the decade, going forward, adding blue sky value as it steps up to the plate. The Roath Branch embankment is alongside the park for its entire run south. It was planted with more than 900 trees in 1910 in order to hide the steam trains and aid the sense of recreation. In their mature form the resultant forest certainly does that.

Splott Park, arguably now in the district of Tremorfa (but we'll let that pass), has an air of industrial otherness hard to experience elsewhere in the city. On the far fringes the green gives way to glimpses of warehouse, industrial unit, smelting plant and other installations of heavy toil. Where are we? The Black Country, the North? This can't be gentle post-industrial sparkling Cardiff, can it? The route bends past the medical centre at the park's southern extremity to repeat the dual bridge experience on South Park Road.

After passing the Lovely Grub café we emerge to face the Grosvenor Hotel. This was built in 1893 but is no longer serving ale nor renting beds. To the south are the marshalling yards of DB Schenker built on reclaimed land that was largely still the sea when the Roath Branch first went by. Keeping to the route of the Roath Branch now becomes more of a challenge than in any of the previous four miles.

Rather than attempt to blag our way through the deeply inaccessible Allied Industrial Park we opt to cross the lesser-green and much rougher feeling Moorland Park. Entrance is via an assembly of metal struts and gates designed to keep anything mechanical out. I feel a bit like a corralled sheep entering a sheep dip. If I was wheelchair bound and wanted a walk in the park then I'd have to go somewhere else.

This brief green is built onto the sites of slum-cleared Lower Splott, the lost streets of Milford, Tenby, Wimbourne, Pontypridd, Llanelly, Caerphilly, and Bridgend. It's a Queen Elizabeth Field, held in trust for the people in celebration of the Monarch's Diamond Jubilee in 2012. The air is clean and bright. It once was not, of course. Standing here at the start of the twentieth century you would see, hear and smell a mighty cross-section of industrial endeavour – brick kilns, Bird and Son's oil and tar distillery, Tharsis Sulphur and Copper Works, metal stampers, enamellers, soap manufacturers, Fownes Forge ship repairs, Bute Gas Works and, mightier than all the rest combined, the fire breathing Dowlais Steelworks. The district was great place in which to sleep and breathe. I came down here on a push bike at the end of the 1950s and even then the noise half scared me to death. How it would have been in health and safety unconscious 1910 is anyone's guess.

We exit south onto Portmanmoor Road. The line has existed since medieval times and it had residential houses along it right up to the 1980s. Shirley Bassey, born in Bute Street, lived here for much of her childhood. Today it is entirely multi-let industrial estate, a component of the great Ocean Park that has replaced the steelworks with light industry, warehouse operations, litho printers, packaging suppliers, manufacturers of windows and doors and all the rest.

We walk south, the Roath Branch running along its spectral tracks to our left. At the Estate's end is the Ocean Way roundabout, a south Cardiff epicentre, a gateway to somewhere and largely not present in the mental roads maps of most Cardiffians. From its rim we look out at the single rail track running from DB Schenker's yards along the one-time bed of the Roath Branch. Here the Taff Vale railway coal carrier terminated in a sprawl of sidings. Of them there is no sign. In their place are timber yards and warehouses. In the distance Hanson's ready-mixed concrete

Celsa Works yard

operation and the EMR scrap metal stacks on Dowlais Wharf. This is the Roath Branch ghost walk's end, I suppose. But busless and with not a café in sight we can't finish here.

It's a relatively short trek across the new road link of Ffordd Ewart Parkinson and a short further stroll along Pierhead Street and Bute Place to the Wales Millennium Centre. In front of us is what's now known as Roald Dahl Plass, a paved over piece of dockland history that was once the Bute West Dock Basin. Here ships waited before entering

Cardiff's first dock, the Bute Ship Canal, which opened in 1834. Today it's a city open space with Barcelona-style street lighting, used for open air food markets, summer funfairs, and an annual visit from the Lady Boys of Bangkok. When its waters were filled in during the late 1960s using waste from the cleared Aberfan coal tips a few bollards around which a lifetime's parade of shipping had been tied were kept. Their metal along with scrap salvaged from Tower Colliery, the last working deep pit of south Wales, was melted and recast by the artist Stefan Gec.

From them he formed the pair of now slowly rusting pit prop-like pillars installed on the Basin's western rim. On one of these are engraved the names of all the pits that exported their coal through Cardiff. On the other are the names of a world of ports to which that coal was sent. As a street artwork 'Deep Navigation' is unsurpassed. There's an intellectual thrill to be had when you first see it and work out just what it is: a post-modern offering that sums up the Cardiff industrial age. It is a testament to a trade which plied its way through this port and in the process made the city. A hundred and fifty years of toil and wealth gone, it seems, in a grime and glowering flash.

At the WMC are toilets, cafés, and warmth. Outside is a stop for the Baycar bendy-bus to the city centre. There's a taxi rank too but if you stroll up Lloyd George Avenue a few hundred metres you'll find Bute Road, now Cardiff Bay, Station. Genuine train tracks right back into the city's focal point (well, Queen Street actually). Most appropriate.

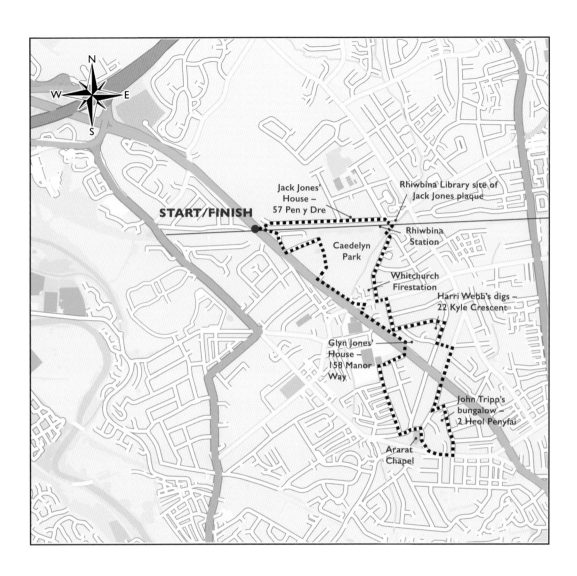

START/FINISH

Jack Jones'
House –
57 Pen y Dre

Rhiwbina Library site of
Jack Jones plaque

Rhiwbina
Station

Caedelyn
Park

Whitchurch
Firestation

Harri Webb's digs –
22 Kyle Crescent

Glyn Jones'
House –
158 Manor
Way

John/Tripp's
bungalow –
2 Heol Penyfai

Ararat
Chapel

20. GLYN JONES' HOUSE TO JACK JONES' HOUSE

A circular walk through Whitchuch and Rhiwbina visiting the former homes of four of Anglo-Welsh literature's big hitters – Glyn Jones, John Tripp, Harri Webb and Jack Jones. This is largely bungalow land with barely a working class terrace in sight. There are cafés on Merthyr Road in Whitchurch and in Rhiwbina village. Public transport is abundant.

Start and finish: Whitchurch railway station
Distance: 3.09 miles
Level

www.plotaroute.com/route/587048

Given that this walk is all about writers it should be pretty bohemian. But actually it's no such thing. When it was fashionable to be Anglo, and believe it or not there was such a time, the writers of the Anglo–Welsh clustered not near the town hubland of winebars and bookshops but in the distant and leafy north Cardiff suburbs. They lived in a land of quiet bungalows and soft-spoken semis where the terrace never reached.

Cae Delyn Park mural, Rhiwbina

Despite the fact that they were often former teachers and librarians and clerks for the government they still regarded themselves as ambassadors for the working class. They were immensely proud of the valleys from which they'd sprung. They wrote about love and loss and the battle against grasping mine owners, strikes, lock-outs, deprivation, desperation and loss. This was a Wales that most Cardiffians simply did not know.

Four of them collected within walking distance of each other in Whitchurch and Rhiwbina. Anglo-Welsh dragons with two tongues. The term Anglo-Welsh had been an invention of the twentieth century. It described writers who came from Wales and were imbued with a Welsh sensibility but nonetheless wrote in English. Its use lasted until at least the 1990s when the rise in national consciousness saw it off. If we don't use the tongue we're all Welsh writers in English now.

It's a breezy day but these are easy streets we are walking through. We climb the steps from the single-track Whitchurch rail station in sight of the water tower of the Hospital. Behind us is the gentle white of Rhiwbina's Garden Village. Tracey Roderick's Mobile Hairdressing and Spark Marky's Kids Disco are its main features, according to Google maps. Ahead is roaring Northern Avenue doing its rush hour best. In the nineteenth century this was a footpath, we take it south.

Mason's Arms carpark

To dilute the diesel we cut into Cae Delyn Park to view the greenness. The changing rooms are embellished with a fire breathing dragon and a mural of parkland very similar to the one we are crossing but with a range of conical volcanos in place of the Caerphilly Mountain ridge. The car park of the Mason's Arms Toby Carvery & Premier Inn beyond the car park is a sea of Sky vans. They must be having a convention

Glyn Jones' house at 158 Manor Way sits behind a giant Leylandii hedge. No Sky dish in his day but there's one now. There is also a plaque giving his dates: 1905-1995. He was the mildest of men. A former teacher from Merthyr Tydfil his novels *The Island of Apples* and *The Valley, The City, The Village* along with his autobiographical critique, *The Dragon Has Two Tongues*, are now much reprinted classics. When he died in 1995 having first lost his right arm to thrombosis he left his house to The Welsh Academy in order to establish a centre for writers. The proceeds from its sale funded the Glyn Jones Centre at the WMC in Cardiff Bay. You can't stay there, as you might have done at Manor Way, but you can explore Welsh literary creativity.

While Glyn was the gentleman of Anglo-Welsh letters the style's enfant terrible was the poet John Tripp. He lived to Glyn's south. We cross the dual carriages of Manor Way, as Northern Avenue is called here. On its far side is a bungalow

land where garden gnome and the ceramic dog rule and plant beds are eternally tidy. Gwaun Tre Oda, Whitchurch Common, is a couple of streets on. Here stands Ararat Chapel. For a time the churchyard held a JT memorial bench giving his name and dates, 1927-1986. But like the bard it's long gone. A great wicker man version of the risen Christ stands in the graveyard's centre with a wicker cross behind.

Tripp, who never attended this church but certainly walked past regularly on his way to the Three Elms, was born in Bargoed in 1927, a fact he shouted out regularly after a few drinks. His public performances of his poetry were legendary. Wales and its history obsessed him. He viewed it through a modernist lens and delighted in the falling from grace of the once great and the failures of the usually successful. Listening to him was an education as much as it was an entertainment.

John Tripp's bungalow, Whitchurch

JT lived with his father at 2 Heol Penyfai, just along from Ararat, almost opposite the plaque which celebrates the American Army planting trees here during World War II. The wrought iron gates of Heol Penyfai residences were largely made by JT's blacksmith father in his forge at Taffs Well. There's no plaque on JT's bungalow. Would Glyn have visited? I doubt it. JT, however, certainly visited Glyn. Glyn's wife, Doreen always complained about how he often managed to arrive at meal times, how long he stayed and how he sometimes left damp patches on their sofa.

We snake on through the low rise landscape of Cae Gwyn Road, Dutch dormers, heart shaped flower baskets, lych-gates, stickers warning against junk mail and plant-filled troughs, to recross Manor Way and, taking the narrow lane next to no 65, pass the only piece of graffiti visible in

Paul Tripp's wrought iron gates, Whitchurch

the entire district. A sprayed tag, hard to see, but evidence of someone with a revolutionary spirit. Not that this is really the right part of the city for the progressive thinker. We are in conservative country. Nevertheless this was where the poet Harri Webb lived in digs for a brief time in the 1960s. 22 Kyle Crescent.

Harri Webb's Kyle Crescent digs, Whitchurch

Harri Webb, (1920-1994), was the great Welsh Republican poet. He was famous for his squib about the first Severn Bridge, "Two lands at last connected / Across the waters wide, / And all the tolls collected / On the English side". Until the Second Crossing opened with its now removed collection booths in Wales this poem was quoted at bridge attendants by disgruntled Welsh lorry drivers. He also wrote 'Colli Iaith' (Losing a Language), which was turned into a song by Heather Jones and sung throughout Welsh Wales. Webb the unrepentant nationalist, the people's poet, "Sing for Wales or shut your trap – all the rest's a load of crap." You'd imagine him as the permanent carouser but he was never that.

We follow Heol Nest and Lon Y Parc to cross to Heol Y Nant and pass Whitchurch Fire Station. If there's a border between Whitchurch and Rhiwbina then it has to be near here. On gate posts half way up stand the slightly larger than life statues of two Middle Earth pugs guarding the frontier. A lane left traverses Rhydwaedlyd Brook and the corner of Caedelyn Park again to cross the railway at Rhiwbina Station.

Inside the library, next to the door to the toilets, is a simple slate plaque commemorating Jack Jones Writer. 1884-1970. Jack, the practical revolutionary, the card-carrying communist, the Labour party member, the speaker at rallies, the agitator. He was miner, a bark stripper, a regular soldier, a speaker for the Liberals, a navvy, an assistant cinema manager and then, finally, a writer. He wrote as he spoke, an unstoppable gush of plot and repartee, thrust and argument, rippling and sparking. He is certainly the most famous of our quartet.

Author of *Bidden to the Feast*, *Off To Philadelphia in the Morning* and *River Out Of Eden,* Jack was a champion of the working class and, in particular, the late nineteenth century working class of the Glamorgan valleys. He was born in Merthyr and came to Rhiwbina almost fifty years later, moving from house to house and then ending up in 1952 at 57 Pen y Dre, a hundred yards west of where his plaque now hangs. How much Jack Jones atmos still hangs in their air? There might have been a time but it's not now. Jack is on the edge of being forgotten. His old and unmarked house is painted Garden Village white and has a black rabbit cut out embellishing its side.

Jones was of an earlier generation than Harri, John and Glyn but, on occasions, they did mix. Jack, the elder statesman, having special bottles of brown ale provided for him at wine consuming literary receptions. He thinks wine is too posh, I was told.

To round the circle we could walk on the short distance down Pen y Dre to reach Whitchurch Station again, where we started. But we don't. We catch the train, like rail-enthusiast schoolboys, all the way to line's end at Coryton and then sit on it the fifteen minutes it takes to roll all the way back to Rhiwbina and then on to Birchgrove and Queen Street in the city centre.

WHAT TO READ NEXT

After *Walking Cardiff,* what to read next? With a few forays into local rurality, the journeys in this book have all been urban walks. They've had a little more depth to their description than is often the case with a guide book. There's a tradition of works like this. At the turn of the millennium the novelist Will Self-published *Psychogeography* (Bloomsbury, 2003), a collection drawn from his column of the same name that ran in the Saturday magazine of *The Independent*.

Here, among many other off-beat adventures, Self suggested a walk from his home south of the Thames all the way to New York. An amazing concept. What he actually meant, of course, was a walk first to Heathrow and then, after flying the Atlantic, a walk from JFK in to Manhattan. But the idea took off.

In the book's introduction Self freely acknowledges psychogeography's origins among the theories of the Lettrist movement and those of Situationist Guy Debord. These artistic reimaginers recalled Baudelaire's notion of the flâneur meandering the city just for the sake of it, the melancholic driven by nothing more than the notion of wandering itself.

In 1995 W.G.Sebald took a walking tour of Suffolk and produced *The Rings Of Saturn*, a tour de force that wove topography and journey with time, memory and notions of identity. The book was published in an English edition in 1998. Quotation marks are absent leaving the reader forever unsure of who is being read.

Iain Sinclair's many psychogeographies, mostly centring on London, are masterly. His *London Orbital* (Granta, 2002) describes a long circular walk following the local hinterlands of the M25. *London Overground* (Hamish Hamilton, 2015) describes a day's walk around what Sinclair dubs the Ginger Line while *Edge of the Orison* (Hamish Hamilton, 2005) follows the footsteps of the poet John Clare escaping both London and his madness.

In *Two Degrees West* (Viking, 1999) Geographer and TV presenter Nicholas Crane tracks this artificial map maker's meridian across 600 kilometres of England from Berwick on the Scottish border to the Dorset sea at the isle of Purbeck. He sets himself rules – he is allowed only to walk and banned from using public or any other sort of transport. He can eat only that which is obtainable inside his self-set corridor of 1000m each side of the line. And if his kit gets lost or damaged – clothes, sleeping bag, river crossing inflatables – then it can only be replaced with material purchased inside his corridor. If there are no stores, which is generally the case, then hard luck. The result is an unrivalled and thoroughly engaging mix of topography, quest, philosophical diversion, history, sociology and high-end journalism. The rules are set and the author reports back on how it went following them.

In my four volumes of *Real Cardiff* I have often described ventures that use similar (although nothing like as restrictive) self-imposed rules. I've walked the length of lost railway lines, followed the vanished Glamorgan Canal, walked rivers which no longer flow, tracked rock and roll's axis along the line formed by Cardiff's now vanished music venues. I've thought about finding a spot determined by rolling dice and then walking every available street and thoroughfare in a one kilometre square centred on that place. I then considered hunting for the location in the city that exhibited, say, the greatest fear. Where could that be? Death junction at the head of City Road, the car park of University Hospital of Wales, the gates of Cardiff Prison? What spirit might still hang in the air?

What I did do was identify the city's psychic centre, discovering in the process just what that meant. You can check it out in *A Cardiff Central Spiral* on page 49.

All of these methods are new ways of experiencing the old. You'll find more in any of Seren's *Real* books as well as in the work of Nick Papadimitriou, Geoff Nicholson, and Stewart Home. Read Lauren Elkin's *Flâneuse: Women Walk the City* (Chatto, 2016). Follow the work of land artist Richard Long whose 1967 *A Line Made By Walking* is a triumph of the flâneur leaving remains of his passage in the landscape. Set your place, throw your dice and go.

NOTES

1. Dérive – an unplanned journey through a usually urban landscape in which participants "let themselves be drawn by the attractions of the terrain and the encounters they find there", as Situationist Guy Debord defines it.

2. Slipper baths were a Victorian invention – a freestanding and slightly shorter than regular bath with one end raised higher than the other. Public slipper baths offered doored compartments behind which the less well-off could privately carry out their ablutions.

3. *Pass the Parcel: Art, Agency, Culture and Community* at Liverpool Biennial 2018, http://www.biennial.com/journal/ issue-5/pass-the-parcel-art-agency-culture-and-community

4. Pre-1923 when the multitude of British rail operators were grouped into the hands of four main companies – the GWR, LNER, LMS and Southern.

5. Sparty Lea – a lead mining hamlet in Northumberland when the MacSweeney family had property.

6. Little Troy – "A garden on the west side of Working Street.....so called after a maze or 'Troy Town' which stood in the Trinity Garden and belonged to St John's church." *Cardiff Records: Volume 5* (1905).

7. When installed the plaque read "Howard Spring, World Famous Novelist 1889-1965. Born at 32 Albert Street, Canton (formerly Edward Street) now demolished".

8. The 1899 visit awarded a crown to R. Gwylfa Roberts but failed to find anything worthy enough to win the chair.

9. Which also housed the miners' Pneumoconiosis Medical Panel

10. See *Real Cardiff #1*

11. A further 160 bed block of Student Accommodation. What else?

12. The Roatherendum was a component of that year's Made in Roath arts festival.

13. They don't. When housing was redeveloped in the Victorian era the spring was "let into the sewers".

14. Bill Nelmes, Director of Parks 1936-1967, Andrew Pettigrew's successor

15. The mile-long Wenvoe Tunnel was opened in 1889 to carry coal on the Barry Railway on to Barry Docks. It closed in 1963.

16. Michell, John, *The New View Over Atlantis*, Thames & Hudson, 1986.

17. A sort of Shazam for birds which runs on your smartphone.

18. Rees, William, *Cardiff A History of the City*, Cardiff Corporation, 1969

19. 'Gelynis' is a corruption of 'Cel-ynys' as the farm is called on early maps. River meadow nook.

20. MX bike track for now. This is the site of a proposed new wood-burning power station.

21. See *Edging The Estuary,* Finch, Peter, Seren, 2013 where Des Barry refers to the Zone in the film *The Stalker* (1979), directed by Andrei Tarkovsky

22. Rumney and District Local History Society, *Rumney and St. Mellons – A History of Two Villages*, Rumney Local History Society, 2005.

23. Best not to get too hung up on names. The official Royal Commission on the Ancient and Historical Monuments of Wales name for this site is *Cae-Castell*. The site is marked as a Roman Camp on the first OS maps. There is a castle site at the top of Rumney Hill, a mile or so distant, which is also known as *Cae'r Castell* and referred to by the Royal Commission as "Caer Castell Ring Motte Rumney". Victorian maps agree on the name but again mark it as a Roman Camp.

24. BISF – British Iron and Steel Federation 'permanent' prefabs constructed in the early 1950s. These are steel-framed three bedroomed domestic dwellings with walls created using steel, lath and render. Enthusiasts have a web site at https://www.bisfhouse.com/latest/

25. The precise site is marked inside the museum and comprehensive maps showing opposing forces and their disposition is on show in a weatherproof case.

26. The first St Marks dated from 1876. It was demolished to build Eastern Avenue. Its replacement opened in 1967 and is just round the corner on North Road.

27. Whitchurch Brook, known further north by its welsh name, Nant Rhydwaedlyd, see p.128

28. This graffiti was painted out the week after we passed by. Zero tolerance in action. But check, memorable new graffiti appears here all the time.

WORKS CONSULTED

Bielski, Alison, *The Story Of St Mellons*, Alun Books, 1985

Billingham, Nigel & Jones, Stephen K., *Images Of Wales – Ely, Caerau and Michaelston-Super-Ely*, Tempus, 1996

Billingham, Nigel & Jones, Stephen K., *Images Of Wales – Ely Common To Culverhouse Cross*, Tempus, 1999

Blanchet, Elizabeth, *Prefab Homes*, Shire, 2016

Bowtell, Harold D., and Hill, Geoffrey – *Dam Builders In The Steam Age – Book Six – Reservoir Builders Of South Wales*, The Industrial Locomotive Society, 2006

Chappell, Edgar L., *Old Whitchurch – The Story of a Glamorgan Parish*, Priory Press, 1945

Chappell, Edgar L., *History of the Port Of Cardiff*, Priory Press, 1939

Childs, Jeff, *Roath, Images of Wales - Splott and Adamsdown*, Tempus, 1995

Cooke, R.A. *Track Layout Diagrams Of The Great Western Railway And B.R. (W.R.) – Section 46B – Pontypridd-Cardiff,* Lightmoor Press, 1996

Davies, Wynford, *Rhiwbina Garden Village – A History Of Cardiff's Garden Suburb*, D Brown & Son, 1985

Gec, Stefan, *Deep Navigation*, CBAT, 2000

Gillham, Mary E., *A Natural History Of Cardiff – Exploring Along The Rivers Rhymney And Roath*, Dinefwr, 2006

Graham, Ken and Taverner, Jim, *Images Of Wales – Rhiwbina*, Tempus, 2004

Hilling, John B. *The History And Architecture Of Cardiff Civic Centre*, UWP, 2016

Hutton, John, *The Taff Vale Railway Volume 2*, Silver Link Publishing, 2006

Jenkins, Stan, *Llanishen – A Historical Miscellany*, Llanishen Local History Society, 2014

Lee, Brian, *Cardiff's Vanished Docklands*, Sutton, 2006

Lee, Brian, *A Cardiff Century – A Capital City For Wales*, Breedon Books, 2004

Morgan, Dennis, *The Illustrated History Of Cardiff's Suburbs*, Breedon Books, 2003

Morgan, Richard, *Place-Names of Glamorgan*, Welsh Academic Press, 2018

Mountford, Eric R., *The Cardiff Railway*, Oakwood Press, 1987

Neal, Marjorie, and others, *Rumney & St Mellons – A History Of Two Villages*, Rumney and District Local History Society, 2005

Newman, John, *The Buildings Of Wales – Glamorgan*, Penguin, 1995

Owen, Hywel Wyn and Morgan, Richard, *Dictionary Of The Place-Names Of Wales,* Gomer, 2007

Radyr And Morganstown New Horizons History Group, *Twixt Chain And Gorge – A History Of Radyr And Morganstown*, Shadowfax Publishing, 1991

Rees, William, *Cardiff – A History Of The City*, Corporation of the City of Cardiff, 1969

Rumney and District Local History Society, *Rumney And St. Mellons A History Of Two Villages*, RADLHS, 2005

Spring, Howard, *The Autobiography of Howard Spring*, Collins, 1972

Swinfen, David, *The Fall Of The Tay Bridge*, Mercat Press, 1994

THANKS AND ACKNOWLEDGEMENTS

Sue, my wife, read the script and made many useful suggestions as well as accompanying me on some of the initial exploratory forays across the city I imagined I knew so well but in the process discovered that I did not. Mick at Seren got excited by the idea, sourced the wherewithal and saw the project through. John Briggs himself became completely involved and took at least six times the number of great photos than those we've ended up including here. The late Meic Stephens recalled in detail the names of those long ago visiting Russians as described in *A Cardiff Counter Culture Poetry Ramble*. Richard Houdmont loaned me books and provided loads of information to help illuminate the Rhiwbina sections. And Cardiff itself which kept on changing, almost every time I looked at it. My obsession. Yes.

PETER FINCH

Peter Finch is a poet, performer, psychogeographer and literary entrepreneur living in Cardiff. He has been a publisher, bookseller, event organiser, literary agent and literary promoter. Until 2011 he was Chief Executive of Literature Wales.

His poetry has been collected in *Selected Later Poems* and *Zen Cymru*, both published by Seren. His *Edging The Estuary,* the story of where Wales becomes England, was published by Seren in the summer of 2013. His *The Roots of Rock: From Cardiff To Mississippi And Back* appeared from Seren in 2016.

He edits Seren's Real series of alternative handbooks, literary rambles and guides to Britain's conurbations. His own *Real Cardiff* (in four volumes) and *Real Wales* have appeared in this series.

His next book will be *The Machineries Of Joy*, poetry from the past decade, to be published in spring of 2020 by Seren

"Since the early 1970s, Finch has been the principal innovator in Welsh poetry...he deserves a Welsh knighthood." – *Richard Kostelanetz, Dictionary of the Avant-Gardes*

"For 40 years he has been the Welsh avant-garde, as inventive and as indispensable as he has been consistently undervalued and ignored...one of the few Welsh writers capable of entrancing young students with his verbal chutzpah, his Crazy Gang of words. Henffych, Peter: a hir oes eto i'ch egni ac i'ch dawn." – *M. Wynn Thomas*

www.peterfinch.co.uk

JOHN BRIGGS

John Briggs is a photographer from Minnesota who has lived permanently in south Wales since the 1970s. As a student at Atlantic College in the mid-1960s he ventured on to the streets of Cardiff with his first SLR. In Minnesota for university in the late 60s and early 70s he worked part-time as a photographer for the *Minnesota Daily*. He returned to Wales in 1974 for teacher training at Cardiff University, taught French in comprehensive schools for 24 years, but also photographed extensively in Cardiff's city centre, docklands and steelworks communities. He is the author of three books published by Seren, documenting the changes that have taken place in Cardiff and Newport over the past four decades. For the past 18 months the experience of photographing for *Walking Cardiff* has often surprisingly, but pleasingly taken him into much unfamiliar territory. In addition to published works, his images have been exhibited widely in Cardiff and Newport.

Published works:

The Pubs of Newport, Handpost Books, 1997. Text by Alan Roderick.

Before the Deluge, Seren, 2002

Taken in Time, Seren, 2005

Newportrait, Seren, 2009

25/25 Vision – Welsh Horizons Across 50 Years, IWA, 2012. Edited by John Osmond and Peter Finch.